M 93/14

D1649849

The Prime Minister

WITHDRAWN

Making Contemporary Britain

General Editor: Anthony Seldon

Consultant Editor: Peter Hennessy

Books in the series

The Prime Minister since 1945

James Barber

BLACKWELL

Oxford UK & Cambridge USA

Copyright © James Barber, 1991

First published 1991

Basil Blackwell Ltd
108 Cowley Road, Oxford, OX4 1JF, UK

Basil Blackwell, Inc.
3 Cambridge Center
Cambridge, Massachusetts 02142, USA

British Library Cataloguing in Publication Data

A CIP catalogue record for this book is available from the British Library

Library of Congress Cataloging in Publication Data

A CIP catalogue record for this book is available from the Library of Congress

ISBN 0-631-17794-9 (hbk.)
ISBN 0-631-17795-7 (pbk.)

Typeset in 11 on 13 pt Ehrhardt
by Setrite Typesetters Ltd, Hong Kong
Printed in Great Britain by Billing & Sons Ltd, Worcester

For the Family
Michael, Andrew, Anne and Mark,
Caroline and Sonia,
and James Patrick

Contents

General Editor's Preface

The Institute of Contemporary British History's series *Making Contemporary Britain* is aimed directly at students and others interested in learning more about topics in post-war British history. In the series, the authors are not attempting to break new ground, but to present clear and balanced overviews of the state of knowledge on each of the topics.

The ICBH was founded in October 1986 with the objective of promoting the study of British history since 1945 at every level. To that end it publishes books and a quarterly journal, *Contemporary Record*, it organizes seminars and conferences for school students, undergraduates, researchers and teachers of post-war history, and it runs a number of research programmes and other activities.

A central belief of the ICBH's work is that post-war history is too often neglected in British schools, institutes of higher education and beyond. The ICBH acknowledges the validity of the arguments against the study of recent history, notably the problem of bias, overly subjective teaching and writing, and the difficulties of perspective. But it believes that the values of studying post-war history outweigh the drawbacks, and that the health and future of a liberal democracy require that its citizens know more about the most recent past of their country than the limited knowledge possessed by British citizens, young and old, today. Indeed, the ICBH believes that the dangers of political indoctrination are higher when the young are *not* informed of the recent past of their country.

Mrs Thatcher's premiership gave sharp focus to the debate about the power of the British Prime Minister. Was the Prime Minister becoming too powerful? Should constitutional checks be brought in to limit that power? Was Britain moving towards a 'presidential' system? These and other questions were regularly posed by journalists and other political commentators. Then suddenly came her fall. In November 1990 the Conservative Party effectively ousted the leader who had won three general elections in a row, and who was regularly being acknowledged as the most influential peacetime Prime Minister this century.

What is needed, therefore, is a book which takes the debate beyond Mrs Thatcher and John Major and looks at the power of the Prime Minister in a longer term perspective. This is the book that James Barber has written, with an analysis of the style and performance of the post-war premiers.

His thematic approach provides far greater insight than a chronological approach would have allowed. Rather than providing a conventional treatment, taking on one Prime Minister after another, Barber has organized his book around subjects which allow one to contrast the different office-holders. These themes include not just policy-making and prime ministerial relations, with party, parliament and Cabinet, but also the structure of the Prime Minister's office and advisers, and the appointment and dismissal of the incumbent of No. 10. It is a book which deserves to be widely read.

Anthony Seldon

Preface

Much has been published about British Prime Ministers. However, usually it has been in the form of biographies and memoirs of individual premiers. Some scholars, journalists and politicians have written about the office of Prime Minister (the premiership) as distinct from the individual holders, and more work is now under way, but such studies are as yet few in number and the academic debate about the premiership is still in embryo.

This short book cannot fill such a large gap, but it does seek to answer some central questions about the office of Prime Minister – 'How do people gain the office?' 'How do they lose it?' 'What part do Prime Ministers play in policy-making?' 'What are their powers?' and so on. Such apparently straightforward questions usually produce less than straightforward answers, if for no other reason than comparisons are difficult to draw. The point is obvious but bears stating, that at any time there is only one Prime Minister (there have only been ten since 1945) and each holds office in different circumstances. Evidence has to be collected and conclusions drawn around the behaviour and experiences of relatively few people in constantly changing conditions.

I am indebted to Anthony King and Anthony Seldon for their valuable comments on a draft of the book; to Cynthia Connolly and Monica Metcalf who prepared the typescript; and to my wife who helped with the bits and pieces that accompany a publication.

James Barber
Hatfield College, Durham University
December 1990

1 The Making

On the evening of 26 July 1945 Clement Attlee, the leader of the Labour Party, was summoned to Buckingham Palace by King George VI. The summons came after Labour's clear and unexpected victory at the general election. Attlee was driven to the palace by his wife Vi in their small family saloon and while she waited outside the King invited Attlee to become Prime Minister and form a government. According to a later report, the conversation between these two shy men started with Attlee saying 'I've won the election', and the King replying, 'I know. I heard it on the Six O'Clock News.'

Having accepted the invitation, Attlee was driven to the Labour Party's victory rally at Westminster Hall. As he passed down the Mall he could reflect with satisfaction that with the war in Europe already over and that against Japan coming to an end, he would be Britain's first post-war Prime Minister. He could also reflect that his new office made him the head of government and the wielder of enormous patronage, including the appointment of the cabinet and other ministers, senior civil servants, the heads of state industries and enterprises, senior positions in the Church of England and chairmen of the government's numerous commissions and bodies. By the end of 1990 nine other party leaders had followed Attlee's footsteps to the palace to become Prime Minister.

Three lessons can be drawn from Attlee's experience at the palace. First, it is the monarch who issues the formal invitation

Table 1.1 Prime Ministers, 1945–1990

Prime Minister	Party	Period
Clement Attlee	Labour	July 1945 – October 1951
Winston Churchill	Conservative	October 1951 – April 1955
Anthony Eden	Conservative	April 1955 – January 1957
Harold Macmillan	Conservative	January 1957 – October 1963
Alec Douglas-Home	Conservative	October 1963 – October 1964
Harold Wilson	Labour	October 1964 – June 1970
Edward Heath	Conservative	June 1970 – February 1974
Harold Wilson	Labour	February 1974 – March 1976
James Callaghan	Labour	March 1976 – May 1979
Margaret Thatcher	Conservative	May 1979 – November 1990
John Major	Conservative	November 1990 –

to become Prime Minister and form a government. Second, by convention the monarch invites the person who is most likely to command a majority in the Commons. Third, the person most likely to command that majority is the leader of the largest party in the House. In short, the Prime Minister is summoned by the monarch, after being chosen by the party which has been elected by the people.

In Attlee's case the King's task was easy because the Labour victory was decisive. It not only formed the largest party but had a clear majority over all others. In other circumstances it can be more difficult and involve the exercise of personal discretion by the monarch. This is the case if an election result is not clear cut; or the leadership of the majority party is in dispute; or the distribution of support in the Commons is uncertain. There were examples of these earlier in the century. In 1923 when Bonar Law, the Conservative Prime Minister, resigned on account of ill health there were two contenders – Lord Curzon and Stanley Baldwin. King George V held the view that the Prime Minister should not be in the Lords, and after consulting Privy Councillors and Tory elder statesmen, he decided 'on the strength of this advice', but also 'in conformity with his personal judgement' to call Baldwin (McKenzie 1963, p. 40). In 1931 the King was active again in persuading Ramsay MacDonald to lead a national government after MacDonald's Labour government had resigned, and MacDonald had lost the leadership of the Labour Party. The King chaired a Buckingham Palace conference which supported a coalition led by MacDonald, and later, when further difficulties arose and MacDonald thought of resigning, the King 'urged him to "brace himself up to realise that he was the only person to tackle the present chaotic state of affairs" that it was his positive duty to find a solution; and that even if Mr MacDonald were to tender his resignation he, the King, would refuse to accept it' (Nicolson 1952, p. 493).

Since 1945, because a predominantly two-party system has prevailed, usually with a clear winner, the monarch has not faced such serious problems. However, two delicate situations have arisen. First, there was dispute over the leadership of the Conservative Party following Macmillan's resignation as Prime Minister in 1963. None of the contenders gained overwhelming party support, and when the Queen summoned Lord Home to the palace he was unable to give an immediate undertaking that he could form a government. There were suggestions that the Queen acted too swiftly — that she should have waited until the situation was clear before summoning Home, for by doing so she gave him an advantage over his rivals, and thwarted an anti-Home movement. However, the Queen did not act on personal judgement but rather on advice within the constitutional convention.

Second, there was confusion following the muddied outcome of the February 1974 election, called by Edward Heath, the Conservative Prime Minister. No party won an overall majority and although Labour was the single largest party, Heath tried to negotiate a pact with the Liberals which would have given him a majority and kept him in power. Denis Healey later claimed that Heath, on the implicit assumption that the monarch was Conservative property, tried to persuade the Queen to invite him to form a government but that only infuriated the palace. Whatever the position, following a weekend of uncertainty, Heath failed to achieve the pact and resigned, advising the Queen to call Harold Wilson, the Labour leader. This she did. After Wilson had formed a minority government, it was suggested to him that immediately after the election the Queen should have called on him to form an administration as the leader of the largest party. Wilson dismissed that view, stating: 'A Government (Heath's) was in existence, and until it resigns, following the election results, or a defeat on the Queen's Speech, the palace can only observe the classical doctrine, "We have a Government"' (Wilson 1979, p. 11).

In 1945, although George VI himself had no doubts about summoning Attlee, there were some Labour leaders who believed that Attlee should not have accepted the King's invitation until he had submitted himself to the party for reselection. Prominent among these were Herbert Morrison, who had ambitions to replace Attlee, and Harold Laski, the party chairman, who emphasized the power of the party outside parliament. Attlee rejected their views. Having led the Labour Party since 1935 and now to an election victory, he had no doubts about his right to form a government, and he accepted the King's invitation without consulting Morrison or Laski. Later (and in contrast with Home in 1963) Attlee said 'if the King asks you to form a government you say "yes" or "no", not "I'll let you know later"' (Harris 1982, p. 263). When Attlee arrived at the party rally in Westminster Hall the unsuspecting Laski introduced him simply as 'party leader', but to the delight of most of his audience, if not the nonplussed Morrison and Laski, Attlee announced that he had just returned from the palace where he had accepted the King's invitation to form a government.

Chosen by the Party

The challenge to Attlee underlined the link between the premiership and the leadership of one of the major parties. Since 1945 these have been the Conservative and Labour parties. The

Conservatives have had seven leaders, Labour six, but while all seven Conservatives have been Prime Ministers, only three Labour leaders have so far formed governments. Of those who have not held the premiership, Gaitskell was elected leader in 1955, and although he lost the 1959 election he was still party leader when he died in 1963; Michael Foot became party leader in 1980, lost the 1983 election and stood down in the same year, to be succeeded by Neil Kinnock, who so far has led the party in opposition, losing the 1987 election.

The demands made on party leaders are many. Put in the form of questions they would include: can they unite the party? can they inspire the faithful? can they bring in fresh public

Table 1.2 Party Leaders and Prime Ministers, 1945–1990

Conservatives

	Party Leader	*Prime Minister*
Winston Churchill	1940–55	1940–5 and 1951–5
Anthony Eden	1955–7	1955–7
Harold Macmillan	1957–63	1957–63
Alec Douglas-Home	1963–5	1963–4
Edward Heath	1965–75	1970–4
Margaret Thatcher	1975–90	1979–90
John Major	1990–	1990–

Labour

Clement Attlee	1935–55	1945–51
Hugh Gaitskell	1955–63	–
Harold Wilson	1963–76	1964–70 and 1974–6
James Callaghan	1976–80	1976–9
Michael Foot	1980–3	–
Neil Kinnock	1983–	–

support? where do they stand ideologically? do they offer new directions and ideas? are they experienced in government? are they competent? can they handle parliament? can they project themselves on the media? can they win elections? In the search for leaders the parties do not consciously use such a check list, but there is a recognition that no person can satisfy all the demands. Therefore the choice has to be a compromise and one which is limited by the candidates who are available. At any time there are only a handful of parliamentarians who are perceived by their party to have the requisite leadership talents and experience. Yet, although few are involved and formal leadership elections are rare, there is constant jockeying for position among potential leaders and regular media speculation about their chances.

The selection of a leader is also influenced by whether the party is in power or in opposition. The Conservative and Labour parties have had different experiences in this respect. Before Wilson's resignation as Prime Minister in 1976, and Callaghan's subsequent election, all Labour leaders had been chosen while in opposition. Following Wilson's decision the *Financial Times* (17 March 1976) wrote of an 'unprecedented event' and 'great confusion over it in Transport House (Labour Party head-quarters)'. In contrast, Eden, Macmillan, Home and Major came to power while the Conservatives were in office and Churchill had done the same when he became wartime Prime Minister in 1940. Before Major's election the Tory pattern had been to gain the premiership first and follow it later with confirmation as party leader. Eden became Prime Minister on 6 April 1955 and party leader by acclamation the day after; Macmillan was Prime Minister on 10 January 1957 and was made party leader on 22 January; and Home in 1963 was Prime Minister for 23 days before being confirmed as leader. (In 1940 Neville Chamberlain had continued for a time as party leader while Churchill was Prime Minister.) The sequence was broken when Edward Heath was elected Tory leader in opposition in 1965. When Heath formed a government in 1970 it was the first time since 1922 that a Conservative Prime Minister had been party leader before becoming Prime Minister. In 1975

Margaret Thatcher followed Heath as Conservative leader in opposition, and then won the 1979 election. In November 1990 Major was elected party leader and immediately succeeded Thatcher as Prime Minister.

When the party is in power, and so is choosing a Prime Minister as well as leader, the advantage lies with a 'safe' candidate, often with experience, who offers stability and unity. When Wilson retired in 1976, Callaghan successfully emphasized these characteristics in a campaign in which he made no electioneering speeches but remained in the public eye through his statesman's role of Foreign Secretary, while his campaign staff underlined his great experience in government and the party. Callaghan himself wrote that he was confident of victory and therefore decided to give no press or television interviews as fellow Members of Parliament were already fully aware of his strengths and weaknesses. An alternative explanation from his critics was that Callaghan was a pragmatist without clear commitments, and therefore decided to avoid debates on policy with men like Benn and Healey.

It is also important that a new Prime Minister can quickly rally the party together behind the government, whereas in opposition there may be more room for internal debate. The rallying together is especially important if the change comes in time of crisis, such as that faced by the Tories in 1956/7 following the aborted invasion of Suez. The party was in disarray. The invasion had misfired, international criticism was heaped upon Britain, and, late in 1956, the sick Prime Minister, Anthony Eden, went to the West Indies in an attempt to recover his health. While Eden was away the two major contenders for his office, Butler and Macmillan, addressed Tory backbenchers (the 1922 Committee). Butler, after a short low-key speech, asked if Macmillan would like to say a few words: 'And the Chancellor did say a few words!' wrote Keith Joseph, 'He peppered his brilliantly effective monologue, if you can apply peppering to silences, with long pregnant silences in which you could have heard a pin drop ... I think that performance was one of the dominating ingredients of the Conservative Party's decision in his favour' (*Contemporary Record* spring 1987). In

November 1990 the Conservatives were in a different but no less severe crisis when a conflict of policy and personality led to the overthrow of Thatcher. In these circumstances the party turned to the safe John Major and not the more ebullient Michael Heseltine.

In opposition, although a party will be hoping to elect a future Prime Minister, the absence of immediate government responsibility gives a breathing space so that greater attention can be given to internal party concerns, less weight to experience in government, and there may be more willingness to take a risk. That was the case when a divided Labour Party elected Michael Foot in 1980. Denis Healey, his main opponent, had greater experience and public prominence, but Foot, who had acquired an elder statesman image and was of 'the left', received more support in the hope of satisfying the party activists and keeping the trades unions happy. Similarly, the Conservatives took a risk in 1975 in choosing Margaret Thatcher, who was relatively inexperienced and who was swept in on a wave of discontent with Heath's leadership. It was, in Julian Critchley's words, a 'peasants' revolt' — as much against Heath as for Thatcher — and it is unlikely that the Tories would have taken the risk had they been in power.

Labour Democracy

The Conservative and Labour parties have made substantial changes in their selection processes since 1945. In both cases the central questions have been who within the party chooses the leader and how is it done. Is it to be a small inner circle, or Members of Parliament, or are local constituencies, affiliated groups and organizations also to be involved? Is it to be an election and if so what kind of election, or a weighing of opinions? In answering these question Labour has prided itself on being more 'democratic' than the Conservatives. It has always elected its leader. Until 1981 this was done by Members of Parliament in the Commons, the successful candidate having to gain a majority of all the votes cast. In 1955 Gaitskell won easily at the first count against Aneurin Bevin and Herbert Morrison. It was not so clean cut on subsequent occasions. For example, when Wilson retired in 1976 there was a prolonged battle among six candidates, which went to three ballots before Callaghan defeated Foot 176 to 137.

There was, however, discontent in some sections of the party in leaving the selection of leader and deputy leader exclusively to Members of Parliament. At the Labour conference in October 1980, after critics had argued that the whole party and not just the parliamentarians should participate, it was agreed to call a special conference to examine the issue. Before that met, Callaghan resigned and in a contest under the old system Michael Foot narrowly defeated Denis Healey. When the special conference met in January 1981 Foot supported the view of Members of Parliament that they should have half the votes in a new electoral college, but that failed to carry the day, and instead it was decided that 40 per cent of votes should go to the trades unions; 30 per cent the constituency parties; and 30 per cent to the parliamentary party. The change was interpreted as a shift to 'the left', and was soon tested when Tony Benn, 'the left's' champion, challenged Healey for the deputy leadership. In the contest Healey, who was supported by most Members of Parliament while Benn had most of the constituencies, scraped home by the narrowest of margins (50.5 to 49.5 per cent). However, when the first full leadership contest was held under the new rules in October 1983 (following Foot's resignation) Neil Kinnock gained a clear majority.

Although the Labour Party has always elected its leaders and the contests have often been bitter, once in office the leaders have enjoyed security. No sitting leader has been defeated in a leadership election or been forced from office: Attlee retired in 1955 full of years; Gaitskell died in office; Wilson retired voluntarily as Prime Minister; and Callaghan and Foot retired while leading the party in opposition. In 1988 Kinnock easily brushed aside a challenge from Tony Benn.

Conservatives Emerging

Before 1965 Conservative leaders 'emerged'. The process was sometimes known as 'the magic circle' − on account of its secrecy and the small number of people involved − and for some Tories it had an almost mystical quality. In 1921 Ernest Pretyman MP declared: 'Great leaders of politics are not elected, they are evolved ... and I think it will be a bad day (when we) have solemnly to meet to elect a leader. The leader is there, and we all know when he is there'. However, he added the very practical consideration that if one voice of doubt is raised 'it will be seized upon and will be magnified into party discussion at a most critical time' (Norton and Aughey 1981, p. 244).

In fact there was considerable variation in the way the 'magic circle' operated, including the part played in it by the outgoing leader. When Churchill handed over to Eden in April 1955 there was no obvious selection process, or even a sounding of party opinion. It was simply assumed that Eden, who had waited long and impatiently in the wings, would succeed. Rab Butler described how Churchill invited Eden and himself into the Cabinet room, where 'we all gazed over Horse Guards Parade. Then Winston said very shortly, "I am going and Anthony will succeed me. We can discuss details later." The ceremonial was over' (Butler 1973, p. 178). There was no adverse reaction in the party to the way Churchill sealed the succession. Churchill declared that 'no two men have ever changed guard more smoothly' (Rhodes James 1986, p. 403).

The change of leadership in 1957 was less smooth. Eden decided to resign following the Suez disaster and his subsequent illness. This time there were rival candidates (Macmillan and Butler) and in a contrast with Churchill Eden played no part in the process. 'If he had a preference,' wrote Robert Rhodes James, 'it was for Butler − and very certainly not for Macmillan − but he was careful not to make any recommendations at all, being a strong believer in the Queen's privilege' (Rhodes James 1986, p. 597). Although Eden resigned because of ill health, he was certainly fit enough to have given an opinion, and even to have participated in the process had he wished. Instead two peers − Lord Salisbury, the leader in the Lords, and the Lord Chancellor, Lord Kilmuir − sounded opinion. They saw individually each Cabinet minister, the Chief Whip, the party chairman and the chairman of the 1922 Committee. No influence was used. Salisbury simply lisped, 'Well, which is it, Wab or Hawold?' There was a clear majority for Macmillan, and when the Queen was informed she sent for him.

The last time a Conservative leader 'emerged' was in 1963. It was a painful, humiliating experience. Macmillan, who had been Prime Minister since 1957, fell ill and announced his resignation from a hospital bed. The announcement coincided with the party conference at Blackpool which immediately was transformed into an arena for a leadership contest as the contenders (Butler, Hailsham, Maudling, Heath, Macleod and Home) paraded themselves. A public and bitter contest ensued. Although Macmillan was ill, he played a key part and let his personal preferences be known − first he favoured Lord Hailsham and later Lord Home, but on one thing he was consistent, he did not want Butler. Macmillan set out the method to be used in giving advice to the Queen. With the Cabinet's approval he arranged for separate polls of the Cabinet, Members of Parliament in the Commons and the Lords, and soundings in constituency parties. When the consultations were complete the Queen came to the hospital where the Prime Minister advised her that Lord Home had the greatest support. (Ironically, Home was able to renounce his peerage and seek a seat in the Commons through recent legislation which he had not supported.) Even after Home had been invited to form a government he did not give the Queen a definite assurance, because several Cabinet members and Members of Parliament (including the other leadership rivals) favoured Butler. Butler was urged to make a stand, but after vacillating he refused and eventually agreed to serve under Home.

Harold Wilson, as Labour leader, made hay of the Tories' discomfort. He spoke of the Conservatives' choosing 'an elegant anachronism' through 'the machinery of an aristocratic cabal'. He pointed out that although the Tories had 350 elected MPs they had failed to find a leader among them, and instead had turned to a man who had not been elected and knew nothing of the day-to-day problems of ordinary British people (Churchill 1964, p. 146). It was following the 1963 contest and the subsequent 1964 election defeat, to which the leadership dispute may have contributed, that the Conservatives decided to elect their leader. The system Home recommended was an electoral college of Tory members in the Commons. To win on a first round a candidate required not only a majority of those eligible to vote but also 15 per cent over all other candidates, thereby ensuring widespread support. If a second ballot were needed, new contenders could stand, and this time a straight majority of all eligible votes was required to win. If that still failed to produce a result there would be a third round based on transferable votes. In exercising their votes MPs were asked to consult Tory peers and their constituency parties.

The system was first put to the test in 1965 when Home resigned and Heath, Reginald Maudling and Enoch Powell were nominated. In the first round Heath gained 150 votes to Maudling's 133 and Powell's 15. Although Heath had failed to gain the required majority plus 15 per cent the other contenders stood down and Heath became leader.

Ten years later the Conservatives had lost three of four elections under Heath, they were again in opposition and Heath, who had never generated warmth, had become increasingly unpopular. However, although the party now had a selection process there was no mechanism for challenging a leader once elected, and it was only under pressure that Heath agreed to revise the system to include an annual reselection, whether or not the party was in power. When Heath agreed to this in 1975 none of his more prominent, experienced colleagues challenged him, partly from loyalty and partly because they believed Heath was a certain winner. William Whitelaw, Heath's deputy, later wrote that he thought a challenge would be a good thing, for Heath would win and 'it would clear the air' (Whitelaw 1989, p. 184). It did more than that. It created the opportunity for Margaret Thatcher to score a surprise victory; first defeating Heath on the first ballot, and on the second sweeping aside a wave of Tory notables, including Whitelaw. It was as much a vote against Heath as for Thatcher, and it is improbable that she would have 'emerged' under the old system. She was an outsider, whose radical views were not widely shared and who had little support in the Shadow Cabinet, the party establishment or the constituencies. Her strength lay among backbenchers, restless at Heath's leadership. Whatever the reason, the Tories had done at their second election what Labour had never done; voted out a leader.

In November 1990 the Conservatives went further when they forced Thatcher from office as Prime Minister. The mechanism which she had used to gain the leadership was now turned against her. Although the opportunity to challenge had been there it was not until 1989, 14 years into her leadership, that Thatcher was opposed, and then by a little-known backbencher, Sir Anthony Meyer. He did not stand as a serious contender for power but to register the discontent that had developed over her policies and style. In the following year Major replaced Thatcher, as described in the next chapter.

Swings and Roundabouts

All the selection methods for leaders have their advocates and critics. Ironically, although Home introduced the Conservative elections, he favoured the old 'magic circle' approach. It had, he wrote, 'almost everything to be said for it. The Whips and the experienced Conservative parliamentarians knew the form of every runner in the field; they knew the Members of Parliament who had to work and live with the chosen leader; and they could operate quickly and quietly in collecting views' (Home 1978, p. 216). It was also claimed (unconvincingly in the light of 1963) that the method avoided overt disputes, because contenders did not campaign against each other, and that it was more sophisticated than the mere counting of heads because it 'weighed' support. The aim was not only to check numbers but the nature and intensity of party feeling. Even a candidate with broadly based support might not be chosen if sections of the party were strongly opposed to him. That probably explains

Butler's fate, for although he had wide support in 1957 and again in 1963 much of it was lukewarm, whereas there were sections of the party which strongly distrusted him.

The election of leaders by colleagues in the Commons has the advantage that Members of Parliament know the candidates, realize that they have to work with them, have a clear understanding of the leader's tasks in government and opposition and through their constituencies are linked to the electorate rather than confined to party activists. The disadvantage is that the Members of Parliament are only one section of the party. To try to counter this the Conservatives, somewhat half-heartedly, asked Members of Parliament to take informal soundings in the constituencies and the Lords, but the Labour Party has taken it much further. Its 1980 system has the advantage of giving a formal voice to all sections of the party, but it has run into strong criticism: first, because of the balance given to the different sections, especially the prominence of the trades unions which it is argued could lose the party votes at a general election; second, because a leader may be imposed against the wishes of Members of Parliament; and finally, because the system may produce a candidate who satisfies party activists but has little appeal to the broader electorate.

Elected by the People

Prime Ministers are made and broken by general elections. In 1945 Attlee was translated from a party leader to Prime Minister because Labour won the election, while Churchill, the great war leader, was consigned to the opposition benches. Failure at elections can lead to loss of the party leadership, as happened to Home who lost in 1964, Heath who lost three elections and Michael Foot who failed in 1983. As table 1.3 shows, Attlee, Wilson, Heath and Thatcher first gained the premiership from opposition; Churchill, Attlee, Wilson, Heath, and Callaghan lost elections as Prime Ministers; and only Churchill and Wilson regained power at subsequent elections. Eden and Macmillan won elections as Prime Ministers, but neither came to office

Table 1.3 Party Leaders and Elections, 1945–1987

		Election Won		*Election Lost*
Attlee	2	(1945, 1950)	2	(1951, 1955)
Churchill	1	(1951)	2	(1945, 1950)
Eden	1	(1955)	0	
Gaitskell	0		1	(1959)
Macmillan	1	(1959)	0	
Wilson	4	(1964, 1966, 1974, 1974)	1	(1970)
Home	0		1	(1964)
Heath	1	(1970)	3	(1966, 1974, 1974)
Callaghan	0		1	(1979)
Thatcher	3	(1979, 1983, 1987)	0	
Foot	0		1	(1983)
Kinnock	0		1	(1987)

nor lost it through elections, and Callaghan always felt in a weak position because he did not have an election victory under his belt. Thatcher has the best electoral record with three wins and no losses. Wilson's is also an impressive performance but he did lose one election and his 'win' in February 1974 was to form a minority government. (Election campaigns are discussed in chapter 5.)

A final element in the making of Prime Ministers is luck. Whatever the individual's abilities or ambitions chance can play a part. It did so when Gaitskell died young to open up the Labour leadership for Wilson; when new legislation enabled Home to renounce his peerage; and when the Tory grandees failed to challenge Heath to give Thatcher her opportunity. Ability, ambition and luck combine to make the Prime Minister.

2 The Breaking

Since 1945 Prime Ministers have lost office in three ways: defeat at a general election (as noted in chapter 1); retirement from a mixture of choice, ill health and party pressure; and loss of support from the parliamentary party.

The precise event, whether it be an election defeat or retirement, is often the final step in a longer process in which the government and/or the Prime Ministers have lost their sense of purpose and/or the confidence of their followers and the electorate. Therefore, while the focus of attention must sometimes be on the Prime Minister as an individual, on other occasions the loss of office is best understood by looking at the government as a whole, or a mixture of the two. Each government faces constant challenges; the test is whether it judges itself and is judged by others to be capable of handling the challenges, or is overwhelmed by them. Governments can be unfortunate in meeting adverse circumstances over which they have no control. For example, in the 1970s the governments of Heath, Wilson (second term) and Callaghan struggled with the consequences of the oil crisis which led to a sharp deterioration in the international economy and inflationary pressures at home. Usually the longer a government stays in power the more the problems pile up, the more its failures become obvious and the more difficult it becomes to maintain its resilience and flexibility in responding to challenges. Therefore, although in all cases of failure the Prime Minister personally must bear some responsibility, the circumstances, and the degree and speed of disintegration vary widely, as illustrated by the examples of Attlee, Eden, Macmillan, Callaghan and Thatcher.

By 1951, after six years in power, Attlee's government was beset by problems: struggling to rule with a small majority, while rising prices and industrial unrest caused discontent at home, and difficulties arose abroad in Iran and Egypt. Within the government, divisions between 'left' and 'right' had been exacerbated by the resignation of three ministers (Bevan, Wilson and Freeman) over the defence budget. Attlee himself was in poor physical shape, suffering from lumbago and sciatica. The government was 'tired and in Attlee's words in later years "out of steam". It was led by an old man who had only just managed to rescue the party from the quarrels that had torn it apart' (Harris 1982, p. 533). Not surprisingly, Attlee's government lost the 1951 election.

Eden's premiership was much shorter and less successful than Attlee's. Eden, an edgy, vacillating man, was constantly interfering in departmental affairs. Even before the Suez crisis some Tories openly criticized his leadership, but it was Suez that overwhelmed him. Lady Eden said she felt as though 'the Suez Canal was flowing through the drawing-room' (Rhodes James 1986, p. 556). The crisis not only overwhelmed the premier, but split the country apart, and left the government so isolated internationally that it was forced to accept an ignominious cease-fire. Eden wilted under the enormous strain. One observer described him: 'Sprawled on the front bench, head thrown back and mouth agape. His eyes inflamed with sleeplessness, stared into vacancies beyond the roof' (Horne 1988, p. 450).

In contrast with Eden, Macmillan's early years were crowned with success. 'Supermac' restored Britain's international position, presided over steady economic growth and won a resounding election victory in 1959. However, from 1961, things fell apart as the government ran into economic problems, leading to an abortive wage freeze. Following that it suffered a series of by-election defeats, failed to gain entry to the EEC and finally ran into spy scandals which culminated in the Profumo affair.

As the troubles mounted Macmillan himself confessed in his diary that he was beginning 'to get very tired ... to lose grip ... much more fatigue'. Far removed from the early days of apparent effortless superiority, Hailsham observed that the Prime Minister 'positively drooled and wasted time ... he was hardly sensible; so often the trouble with a man when his powers are failing' (Horne 1989, p. 529).

Callaghan also enjoyed success for much of his premiership, and looked firmly in control until the 'winter of discontent' of 1978—9. Then his government broke as its economic and industrial policies were destroyed by militant union power. 'Ministers', wrote an adviser at No. 10, 'were clearly demoralized. Moving among them as they gathered for the cabinet in the hallway outside the Cabinet room, their sense of collective and individual depression was overwhelming', and the Prime Minister was 'worryingly lethargic. He was clearly very tired, both physically and mentally' (Donoughue 1987, pp. 176—7). Callaghan later wrote that for three years

> we had believed in ourselves and in our capacity to govern and to win, despite the odds against us. Now I sensed this was no longer true. Nearly thirty years earlier, as a junior minister in the Attlee Government, I had watched demoralization set in and a thick pall of self doubt begin to envelop ministers as they and the increasingly paralysed Government Departments and Civil Service waited for the inevitable election. (Callaghan 1987, p. 561)

Thatcher dominated British politics for more than a decade, scoring three successive election victories and exercising powerful personal leadership in a government of the 'radical right'. Yet by 1989 and 1990 her government was in serious difficulties: split apart over Europe, saddled with the deeply unpopular poll tax, trailing well behind the Labour Party in opinion polls, faring badly in local elections and parliamentary by-elections. There was increasing criticism of Thatcher herself and her authoritarian, belligerent style. Late in 1989 the Chancellor of the Exchequer, Nigel Lawson, resigned over differences with her, and he was followed a year later by

Geoffrey Howe, the Deputy Prime Minister. These divisions and tensions were the setting for the challenge to Thatcher's leadership.

Resignations

Five Prime Ministers have resigned in office: Churchill, Eden, Macmillan, Wilson and Thatcher. Wilson's is the only absolutely clear-cut case, when the choice was made personally by the Prime Minister without any form of pressure. When Wilson announced his retirement in March 1976 it came as such a surprise, not least to most of the Cabinet, that there was suspicion that there must be 'more to it than meets the eye'. However, Wilson had planned the move. After winning the two elections in 1974 he decided that he would retire near his sixtieth birthday. He gave four reasons for this: first, he had been party leader for 13 turbulent years with eight as Prime Minister; second, if he remained there was a danger of repetition, of failing to see new options and giving fresh consideration to problems; third, he wanted to give somebody else among the Labour team the opportunity to lead; and finally, the new leader should have the chance to establish himself before the next election. In addition, Wilson appeared to be bored with government and with the bickering of the Labour Party. 'I have been round this racetrack so often', he said, 'that I cannot generate any more enthusiasm for jumping any more hurdles' (Donoughue 1987, p. 11).

Although the next three resignations rested on personal decisions, and in the cases of Eden and Macmillan involved ill health, there are question marks against each of them. To a greater or lesser degree the resignations were forced. Although Churchill chose his own moment to go in 1955, it came after persistent pressure to make way for Eden. When he came into office in 1952, aged almost 77, Churchill told his secretary, John Colville, that he would probably only serve for one year. However, to Eden's frustration, Churchill found reason after reason to stay on – to organize a summit, to take advantage of the situation following Stalin's death, to help the new Queen.

He continued to serve despite a heart attack in 1953, despite failing powers, despite Eden's obvious resentment and despite direct pleas from senior Tories. In 1952 Buchan-Hepburn, the Chief Whip, had the unenviable task of conveying a message to Churchill that his colleagues thought he should consider standing down, and in 1954 Macmillan undertook the same task via Lady Churchill. Neither succeeded (Seldon 1981, p. 48). By the winter of 1953–4 Colville wrote of Eden's 'hungry eyes' becoming more beseeching and impatient. In December 1954 Churchill told a tense Cabinet: 'I know you are trying to get rid of me ... but I won't [go].' He said that if ministers were dissatisfied they could hand in their resignations and face an election, but he would tell the public what had happened (Hennessy and Seldon 1987, p. 85). When Churchill finally decided to retire in 1955 it was not linked to ill health or directly to the prompting of colleagues but the realization that his summit proposals had come to nothing. Even then he managed to feel resentment. 'The ensuing days', wrote Colville, 'were painful. Winston began to form a cold hatred for Eden, who, he repeatedly said, had done more to thwart him and prevent him pursuing the policy he thought right than anybody else.' Churchill claimed that the only reason he was retiring was for Anthony (Colville 1985, p. 706).

Eden himself resigned after less than two years. A major reason, but not the only one, was ill health. Eden came to office with a chronic health problem which intensified during Suez. Before the crisis was over and while British troops were still on the canal, Eden, advised by his doctors, took a long holiday in the West Indies. Shortly after his return he resigned. A number of explanations have been advanced for this. One is that it was simply ill health and nothing more, that Eden was eager to continue but his condition was so serious that he accepted the medical advice that he would kill himself if he went on. Other explanations rest on a combination of ill health, which was not in doubt, and pressure. These include the view that the acute ill health was itself a product of the stress associated with Eden's poor showing, and David Carlton has even suggested that the medical advice given to Eden was flavoured by the political judgement that he should go (Carlton 1988, pp. 93–4).

While Eden was away, Butler and Macmillan had set out to organize the withdrawal of British troops from Suez and to repair relations with the US, and in looking to the future they may both have concluded that the government and the party would be better off without Eden and under their own leadership. When Eden returned on 14 December 1956 he was looking well and apparently intent on remaining Prime Minister. However, his poor standing, together with mounting rumours of collusion with the Israelis and the increasing realization of Britain's humiliation, were soon brought home to him. When he returned to the Commons only one Conservative backbencher cheered and waved his order paper, underlining the doubts of the rest. Eden's Commons speeches failed to improve the situation, and under pressure at a meeting with Tory backbenchers he lied about collusion. By Christmas he was voicing doubts about continuing as Prime Minister and after further consultation with his doctors he resigned on 8 January. As Richard Lamb wrote: 'How far this was due to his health, the state of mind of his colleagues, the impossibility of keeping collusion secret, or the realisation of the extent of the failure of his Suez policy, will never be known' (Lamb 1987, p. 304).

Elements of uncertainty also surround Macmillan's resignation. Although his medical problems were less serious than Eden's, ill health was again given as the reason for resignation. As noted above, Macmillan's early years were crowned with success but as pressure mounted in the early 1960s he started to consider resignation. During the summer of 1963 he regularly reflected on whether to give up the premiership and who should replace him. At one stage he concluded that he should resign to give time to a successor to establish himself before an election, but at the beginning of October, as things started to improve for the government, he decided to stay and fight another election. Then the prostate problem arose.

Without doubt, Macmillan was in agony. However, perhaps because of mental or physical malaise, he put the gloomiest interpretation on the immediate advice he received from the doctors he consulted (his own doctor was away) and announced the resignation before the prostate operation. When his own doctor returned, before the operation, he advised Macmillan that he would be able to continue afterwards, and a few days after the operation the doctor prepared a memo on the Prime Minister's instructions which stated that Macmillan would be able 'to lead the party in six weeks' time, and that he can do the work of the Premier at Downing Street within a few days of his return there.' By then, however, although the operation was a complete success, the pass had been sold. The view of Macmillan's biographer, Alistair Horne, is that Macmillan was predisposed to put the worst views on things (Horne 1989, p. 542). It is reasonable therefore to ask whether Macmillan would have resigned if he had been enjoying a period of personal popularity and/or his government had been in a confident mood instead of the uncertainty that remained after the previous criticism and even ridicule.

Criticism and pressure therefore played a part in the resignation of three Conservative Prime Ministers, but, as Churchill's case had revealed, there were great difficulties under the old arrangements of removing a leader who was determined to hold unto office. In all three cases the leaders eventually jumped even if they had been given encouraging pushes. However, that was before the introduction of Tory leadership elections in 1965, and, even more ominous for the leaders, the annual opportunity to challenge which was introduced in 1975. That led first to the downfall of Heath, and then, in one of the most dramatic episodes of recent British politics, to the overthrow of Thatcher in 1990. The difficulties which had increasingly beset the Thatcher government have been sketched out above, but it was not until 1989 that her leadership was first challenged, and then only by Sir Anthony Meyer.

The significant clash followed in 1990. However, for most of that year it appeared unlikely that her leadership would be challenged, if only because a general election had to be held within two years and most in the party wanted to avoid a divisive leadership struggle. The situation changed dramatically in November when the Deputy Prime Minister, Geoffrey Howe, first resigned from office and then attacked the Prime Minister in the Commons. Rejecting assertions that he only differed with Thatcher over style, Howe identified differences of policy and attitude. He spoke of a tragedy for the party, the government and for the Prime Minister herself in her dealings with the European Community which had created a serious risk for the whole nation. He concluded that: 'The time has come for others to consider their own response to the tragic conflict of loyalties with which I have myself wrestled for perhaps too long.' The gauntlet that Howe threw down was picked up by Michael Heseltine who six years earlier, after clashing with Thatcher, had walked out of the Cabinet. Since then Heseltine had nursed his ambition to lead the party, and, although he would probably not have chosen 1990 as the best time to strike, had he failed to do so after Howe's call he would have been accused of cowardice.

A short and bitter leadership campaign ensued, revealing deep divisions among Tory MPs. Thatcher accused Heseltine of being a pseudo-socialist and threatened to resign if he won. Heseltine did not win, but on the first round he gained 152 votes to Thatcher's 204 with 16 spoiled papers. Although Thatcher had a clear majority she had just failed to gain the requisite 15 per cent clearance over her opponent. Characteristically she immediately declared that she would fight on in the second round and win. But she had been damaged beyond repair. Although she had gained a majority of votes the substantial number of MPs who opposed her − despite pressure from constituencies and a natural loyalty to the leader − underlined her inability to unite the party in parliament. Recognizing that she was fatally wounded, most of her Cabinet, having backed her in the first round, now told her that there was no hope of victory, that a tide was running against her and she would lose the second ballot. Some advised her to withdraw with dignity. Thatcher, a fighter by instinct, recalled her three election victories and the majority she had gained on the first round, but reluctantly took the advice and withdrew, commenting that 'It's a funny old world.' Although technically she had resigned, in reality she had been driven from office.

Thatcher's withdrawal created an opening for John Major

and Douglas Hurd (the senior ministers who previously had nominated her) to stand for the leadership. They had the advantage over Heseltine of being able to offer themselves as candidates who would heal the party's rifts, and in fact all three candidates ran campaigns which were remarkably free of personal acrimony. Heseltine already had his organization in place but Major's backers had anticipated the situation and quickly had their campaign running, backed by the party's right wing who wanted to block Heseltine and thought that Major was the most likely to preserve the Thatcher heritage, a view endorsed by Thatcher herself who actively campaigned for Major. Hurd, although supported by most of the senior Cabinet ministers had a less dynamic campaign, and with the sniff of success in the air members rallied to Major as the man who could reunite the party. At the second ballot Major gained 185 votes, Heseltine 131 and Hurd 56. Although Major was two short of a straight majority Heseltine and Hurd immediately declared their support for him, thereby making a third ballot unnecessary. Thus a leadership election which began in great bitterness ended with a degree of harmony and a new sense of life for the Conservatives.

3 The Social and Political Moulding

'Moulding' is interpreted here in two ways. In this chapter, by examining the social and political experiences of Prime Ministers, and in the next chapter by the way in which the public image of Prime Ministers have been 'moulded' by the media.

From Marble Halls to Grocer's Shop

In class-conscious Britain one of the most striking changes among Prime Ministers since 1945 is unrelated to party or ideology. It is social background. Until 1964 post-war Prime Ministers (categorized by their fathers' occupations) were drawn from the upper and professional classes, and were educated at private schools. Even the Labour leaders had professional, middle-class backgrounds, with public school education — first Attlee, and then Gaitskell (who was party leader but not Prime Minister). The first four Conservative Prime Ministers — Churchill, Eden, Macmillan and Home — all came from aristocratic families. However, during 'the swinging sixties' aristocratic leaders looked increasingly anachronistic, and none more so than Alec Douglas-Home, the most charming of all post-war Prime Ministers, but a man out of his time. Even Tory supporters despaired as Home replaced Macmillan. 'We are sick', one said, 'of seeing old-looking men dressed in flat caps and bedraggled tweeds stalking with a 12 bore' (Norton and Aughey 1981, p. 144).

Table 3.1 Social class

	Father's work/Position	Social category/status
Attlee	solicitor	professional/middle class
Churchill	duke, politician	aristocrat
Eden	baronet, landowner	aristocrat
Macmillan	viscount, publisher	aristocrat
Home	earl, landowner	aristocrat
Wilson	chemist	skilled artisan
Heath	carpenter/builder	skilled artisan
Callaghan	naval petty officer	skilled artisan
Thatcher	grocer	shopkeeper
Major	vaudeville artist	skilled artisan

Home's fall from power in 1964 was a social watershed for Prime Ministers. He was replaced by Wilson who became the first in a line of Prime Ministers who were children of lower middle class and skilled workers and who were educated at state schools. The contrast was brought home later by Major, who, writing in 1980, ten years before he became Prime Minister, stated: 'I did neither attend public nor private school nor Oxbridge − nor indeed any university. I did not inherit wealth or marry it' (Daily Telegraph, 28 November 1990).

As Major's statement and tables 3.1 and 3.2 illustrate, the education of Prime Ministers is closely related to social class, with a sharp division from private to state schools from the time Wilson succeeded Home. Wilson was the first of 'the grammar-school generation', who, like other children from the working and lower middle classes used the grammar schools as a ladder for upward mobility. Whatever their other differences, Wilson, Heath and Thatcher had remarkably similar educational backgrounds − grammar school and university. Neither Callaghan nor Major (like Churchill before them) went to university, but, while Major attended a grammar school (where he failed to shine and left at 16), Callaghan is an exception in the sense that his was not a grammar school.

Table 3.2 Education

	School	University
Attlee	Haileybury (private)	Oxford (University College)
Churchill	Harrow (private)	–
Eden	Eton (private)	Oxford (Christ Church)
Macmillan	Eton (private)	Oxford (Balliol College)
Home	Eton (private)	Oxford (Christ Church)
Wilson	Wirral Grammar (state)	Oxford (Jesus College)
Heath	Chatham House (state)	Oxford (Balliol College)
Callaghan	Portsmouth Northern (state)	–
Thatcher	Kesteven and Grantham Girls (state)	Oxford (Somerville College)
Major	Rutlish Grammar School, Wimbledon	–

Equally striking in the educational profiles is the dominance of Oxford as a university. Irrespective of party or class, the seven post-war Prime Ministers who attended university all went at Oxford. Of these two (Attlee and Home) studied history, two others (Wilson and Heath) philosophy, politics and economics, Eden graduated in oriental languages, and Macmillan in the Classics. Thatcher alone studied science and later she qualified in law.

Thatcher was also distinctive as the only woman ever to become Prime Minister. She broke the male monopoly with a vengeance in holding the office longer than any other twentieth-century Prime Minister. However, she was not identified in any way with 'women's liberation' and in her time no other woman held a Cabinet post.

Political Experience

Another major influence is political experiences prior to gaining the premiership. These include: their ages on entering parliament, on entering the Cabinet and on gaining the premiership; their ministerial experience before entering No. 10; and their length of service as Prime Minister.

Table 3.4 reveals that all Prime Ministers have held Cabinet posts before gaining the premiership but the range of experience has varied greatly. The least experienced have been Wilson and Thatcher in terms of offices held, and Major in terms of length of Cabinet service; the most experienced Churchill and Callaghan. Only Callaghan had held the three most senior Cabinet posts under the Prime Minister – Foreign Secretary, Chancellor of the Exchequer and Home Secretary. Of the great offices of state, five future Prime Ministers had been Foreign Secretaries (although Major held the office for only three months), four Chancellors of the Exchequer and two Home Secretaries.

Impact of Office

Undeniably, the office of Prime Minister is demanding and stressful. Reflecting on his time as Prime Minister, Wilson said that the greatest personal asset required was the ability to sleep well. Some of the holders (Eden and Macmillan) left office from ill health, which, at least in part, was caused by the strains of office, and others (Attlee and Callaghan) gave the impression of being exhausted when they reached the end of their tenure. This is hardly surprising with the constant pressure of office, and the fact that most Prime Ministers have come to office in middle age (the average age on gaining office being 59, as noted in table 3.3).

Common descriptions of the Prime Minister's life are of 'pressure', 'strain', 'overwork', and 'loneliness'. James Margach, a veteran reporter, claimed that 'of the dozen (Prime Ministers) I have known at first hand, far too many left No. 10 Downing

Table 3.3 Age and experience

	Age on entering parliament	Years in Cabinet before premiership	Age as PM	Period as PM (yrs/mths)
Attlee	38	8	62	6.3
Churchill	25	17	76*	3.6*
Eden	26	14	58	1.9
Macmillan	30	7	62	6.9
Home	28	12	60	1.0
Wilson	29	4	48	7.9**
Heath	34	5	54	3.8
Callaghan	33	8	64	3.2
Thatcher	34	4	54	11.6
Major	36	3	47	
Average (1945–90)	31	8	59	5.1

* This excludes Churchill's wartime premiership.
** Wilson had two spells as Prime Minister.

Table 3.4 Cabinet posts held before premiership

Attlee	Postmaster General; Lord Privy Seal; Secretary of State for Dominions; Deputy Prime Minister
Churchill	Home Secretary; Secretary of State for War; Chancellor of Exchequer; First Lord of Admiralty
Eden	Lord Privy Seal; Foreign Secretary; Leader of Commons
Macmillan	Minister of Housing; Secretary of State for Defence; Foreign Secretary; Chancellor of Exchequer
Home	Secretary of State for Commonwealth; Leader of Lords; Foreign Secretary
Wilson	President Board of Trade
Heath	Chief Whip; Minister of Labour; Lord Privy Seal (Foreign Office); Secretary of State for Industry and Trade
Callaghan	Chancellor of Exchequer; Home Secretary; Foreign Secretary
Thatcher	Secretary of State for Education
Major	Chief Secretary to Treasury; Foreign Secretary; Chancellor of Exchequer

Street physical and nervous wrecks.' One of the reasons, he suggested, was that 'they never knew when they were at their peak, when to make the exit in dignity, honour and even glory. By desperately holding on too long, they were overtaken by the lengthening shadows of eventide' (Margach 1981, pp. 39–40).

Table 3.5 The longevity of post-war Prime Ministers

Age of Prime Ministers who have died		*Age of those still alive (1 January 1991)*	
Attlee	84	Home	87
Churchill	91	Wilson	74
Eden	80	Heath	74
Macmillan	92	Callaghan	78
		Thatcher	65
		Major	47

Certainly there are problems of staying in office too long. Contenders for such criticism are Attlee, Churchill, Macmillan and Thatcher. One danger for all Prime Ministers is increasing isolation from the rough-and-tumble of political life, because, from choice or circumstance, they become surrounded by those who are too deferential or out of touch with sentiments in the party and the country. Another is that Prime Ministers, already middle-aged on taking office, outstay their generation. For example, both Churchill and Macmillan were nine years older than anybody else in their Cabinets when they retired, and when Thatcher was forced from office not one of her original Cabinet remained in government.

Yet despite all the strain, the pressure, the loneliness and the accusation of staying on too long, the Prime Ministers who have held office since 1945 have shown remarkable longevity, and it must be said of Thatcher in particular she seemed as full of energy and drive as ever when she left office after more than 11 years.

4 The Media Moulding

Politicians and the media rely on each other and distrust each other. The media (broadcasting and press) help to set the political agenda, identify priorities within that agenda, interpret political events, provide the public with their main source of news and opinion and offer channels for political leaders to convey their views and be examined on them. They also create images of political leaders. Prime Ministers, like all politicians, want attention, and the media are eager to give it to such major figures, but while Prime Ministers hope to be treated with understanding and to have their views reported sympathetically, the media want to question, investigate and criticize. Each side therefore tries to mould the other, and it is through the media, whether it be political reports, interviews, cartoons or satirical television programmes, that the public builds its picture of a Prime Minister.

The media's importance is reflected in the determined efforts most Prime Ministers have made to manage them. There have been two exceptions, Attlee and Home. Attlee made low-key radio broadcasts, ignored the infant television and saw the press less in political terms than as satisfying his personal interests (cricket scores and crossword puzzles). Home found the idea of 'selling' himself distasteful. However, they were exceptions and were criticized in their own parties for failing to project themselves. In contrast, most Prime Ministers have made extensive efforts to use the media through such devices as personal contacts, the lobby system, professional advisers and controlled leaks. James Margach accused Churchill of using 'the majesty of office to steam-roller Fleet Street' (Margach 1978, p. 64). Yet a balance has to be struck. While Attlee and Home were criticized for not projecting themselves enough, others, like Wilson, were criticized for trying too hard. Such criticism has usually come from political opponents, but there can also be resentment from colleagues. In 1961, Selwyn Lloyd, the Chancellor of the Exchequer, wrote indignantly to Macmillan:

> I get the feeling that those who conduct your public relations think that it strengthens your position for it to be thought that you are controlling and directing in minute detail every aspect of Government effort . . . . If I am right about this feeling that it is thought important to 'boost' the Prime Minister I suspect that it is the worst possible tactic. The idea that you are preparing the Budget . . . does not in my view enhance your prestige. (Thorpe 1989, p. 322)

Despite such criticism, efforts to 'boost' the Prime Minister increased steadily over the period, so that by the 1980s Thatcher was using a range of professional advisers to project her image.

All Prime Ministers have appointed press secretaries, most have used speech writers and with the growth of television professional advisers have become increasingly important. Yet the personality of the Prime Minister always comes through. Churchill wrote many of his own speeches. When a bemused US President Eisenhower asked his aides how Churchill could possibly publish speeches about their meeting as soon as his plane landed in Britain he was told that Churchill 'rolls his own'. Heath did not 'roll his own' and infuriated his advisers by not paying attention to their drafts until the very last moment so that his speeches were often no more than adequate. In contrast Thatcher worked hard on her speeches and closely with her advisers. The aim of the advisers, especially in tele-vision, is to emphasize attractive individual characteristics and play down those that are less appealing. Douglas Hurd, who was Heath's political secretary, said that Heath's team of advisers 'were not out to create something called the new Heath, smooth, homogenized and empty. What we were trying to do was to help Mr Heath build on the strengths of communication which he naturally possessed.' These were considerable, especially when he had personal contact with a small group, but, said Hurd 'introduce a rostrum, a microphone, an interviewer ... and the result could be disastrously different .... . Instead of speaking to people, Mr. Heath would too often speak at them.' The aim of the advisers, which did not succeed in Heath's case, was to counter that change (Hurd 1979, pp. 72–3).

Another form of management is the way Prime Ministers have 'leaked' information to suit their purposes. When Eden came to power he already knew that Churchill used his contacts to influence newspaper proprietors, but he was surprised to discover that Churchill also leaked confidential information to some of the press. Such behaviour is not uncommon and is little more than an addition to the formalized 'lobby system' by which a limited number of accredited journalists are given unattributable briefings by the government. The journalists 'depend on briefings that supposedly never take place with government spokesmen who do not officially exist'. Sometimes the Prime Minister will personally brief correspondents, but more usually the press secretary ('a source close to the Prime Minister') is the main channel. Bernard Ingham was so close to Thatcher that: 'It's as if', wrote a lobby man, 'you are talking to the Prime Minister herself' (Cockerell, Hennessy and Walker 1984, pp. 10, 69). The lobby system has been criticized not only for its secrecy but its occasional misuse. For example, in 1977 Callaghan's press office tried to discredit the British Ambassador in Washington (whom Callaghan wanted to replace) by describing him as a 'fuddy-duddy' and 'old-fashioned snob', and Thatcher used the lobby to attack members of her own Cabinet via Bernard Ingham. In opposition some party leaders have spoken against the system, and occasionally Prime Ministers, resentful of their treatment, have temporarily abandoned it, as Churchill did in 1951 and Wilson in 1975. Yet, the system has survived because unattributable briefings are advantageous both to the media and to the government.

If Eden was surprised at the leaking of information, he personally suppressed information of collusion with Israel at Suez in 1956. Suppression of information has been associated with matters which in the government's eyes concern the security of the state (e.g. nuclear weapons and the security services) and national prosperity (e.g. the sterling exchange rate), but it is difficult to draw lines between such legitimate concerns and the government's political advantage. Sometimes political advantage has predominated — for example when both Labour and Conservative governments suppressed the rising cost of Concorde, and in 1983 when the 'wets' in the Cabinet overruled Thatcher on a 'Think Tank' report on reducing social service provision. In these, as in other matters, the government enjoys an advantage. Lord Radcliffe, commenting on the press in 1976 concluded that the government

> have all the resources of modern public relations at their beck and call. They have all the subtle art of pressure, the nods and winks, the smile at what is called the responsible reporter and the frown at the man who does not see quite clearly the government's point of view. There is nothing evil about this. But it is one of the conflicts that goes on between the government — whatever government it is — and the press who are seeking to do their duty of telling the public the news. (Radcliffe 1976)

Yet, the advantages are certainly not all one way. First, the government's political opponents also use the media, and second the 'duty of telling the public' is interpreted by many journalists and interviewers as an exploration of the government's problems and weaknesses, and by some as a means of demonstrating their hostility to those holding power. The mutual dependence and tensions were noted by Nora Beloff, a political columnist. She confessed: 'I was paid to keep a close watch on what went wrong in Westminster and Whitehall,' based on the journalistic assumption that 'what is right is never news.' It is in that stressful context that she came to know politicians. While Heath was leader of the opposition Beloff accompanied him on a tour of the Far East, but later when she was given the task of covering the 1970 election, she decided (wrongly as it transpired) that Wilson would win and spent most of her time with him.

Whenever she joined Heath he would bow, mock heroically, and say, 'Fancy you here, what an honour.' Beloff's troubles were not confined to Heath. As the first correspondent to comment on the influence exercised on Wilson by his 'kitchen cabinet' and in particular Marcia Williams, Beloff was treated with distrust by Wilson. He described her as this 'dangerous woman', tried to isolate her from contact with colleagues and at one period had her followed to check on her contacts (Margach 1978, pp. 147–8).

On a more positive note, Beloff also revealed the way Prime Ministers try to establish favourable channels of communication. In the 1960s when she was writing about Britain's attempts to join the EEC, Macmillan did not have time to see her but he authorized his principal private secretary to help. Beloff discovered that the secretary was an old friend, and, with the unrecognized compliance of Macmillan, she renewed a relationship through which she discussed virtually every political story of the day. When Home succeeded Macmillan the friend's period at No. 10 was coming to an end but Home retained the channel by introducing Beloff to the new secretary (Beloff 1973, pp. 187 and 203–5).

The Media's Changing Face

There have been great changes in the media, mainly, but not exclusively, related to the rise of television. Radio and the press have continued to play significant parts in setting the political agenda and providing comment and debate, but television has become the major element. Alongside that there has been a clear change of style in political reporting away from the relative deference of the 1940s and 1950s. A remarkable example of deference came in 1953 when the press and BBC agreed to suppress news of a stroke which had incapacitated Churchill. It is inconceivable that such reticence would have been exercised later. In terms of political allegiance there have also been changes in the press in favour of the Conservatives. In 1950 half the press supported the Tories and 40 per cent Labour, whereas by 1987 the Tories had 70 per cent of the press and Labour only 25 per cent (Butler 1989, pp. 94–5). Also, a clear gap emerged between the 'serious' newspapers and the 'tabloids', although ironically both adopted styles which put increased pressure on political leaders. While the serious press developed investigative journalism the tabloids went in search of sensations and scandals.

The major development, however, has been in television. Neither Attlee nor Churchill gave television broadcasts as Prime Ministers and refused the opportunity when offered. 'Why?' asked Churchill, 'Do we need this peepshow?' At that time political coverage on television was so restricted that not only did the Prime Ministers refuse to appear, but no subject likely to be debated in parliament within a fortnight was allowed to be discussed, and television played little part in elections. Change started in the 1950s: Independent Television was founded in 1954; Eden was the first Prime Minister to use television (in set-piece talks and scripted interviews); and by 1955 38 per cent of households had sets. However, it was during Macmillan's premiership, in the late 1950s and early 1960s, that television really came into its own. There was a rapid increase in the viewing public so that by 1964 90 per cent of households had sets. Conventions also changed: 'the 14-day rule' was dropped; political interviews became commonplace; and while Eden had prearranged his interviews Macmillan walked naked into shows like 'Tell the People' and 'Press Conference'. He emerged as the first Prime Minister with a strong television image — that of an unflappable, clubbable Edwardian — and he became adept at using television at elections and on his overseas trips.

In contrast, Home, who succeeded Macmillan, was inept on television. 'I fear', he wrote, 'I could not conceal my distaste for the conception that the political leader had also to be an actor on the screen' (Home 1978, p. 201). Conscious of his own limitations, he tried to play down television, but his failure only served to underline its importance. Home's opponent, Wilson, made no such mistake. He recognized the importance of the media in general and television in particular, and courted correspondents and producers in a conscious effort to build his image. When he first came to power he presented himself as a young vigorous leader committed to technological advance, and when he returned as premier in 1974 he cultivated the image of the elder statesman. Wilson also demonstrated the importance of timing and brevity by using 'sound bites' timed to catch the television news bulletins, and he was not above upstaging opponents. In October 1965, for example, he diverted attention from the Tory conference by making a broadcast on Rhodesia, and then making a dramatic, if unnecessary, dash to Balmoral to consult the Queen.

Although in his time Wilson was an able television practitioner such was the pace of change that Joe Haines (Wilson's press secretary) later wrote: 'Harold and I were a couple of TV amateurs. We were like the man with the red flag walking in front of the motor car compared with Mrs Thatcher's highly professional publicity advisers today' (Haines 1977, p. 226). By the 1980s all political leaders recognized the importance of television. 'You don't need to tell me what to do,' said Neil Kinnock, 'I got to be leader of the Labour Party by being good on television,' and when he came to fight his first election as leader in 1987 Kinnock used television to create new images of himself and the Labour Party (Cockerell 1988, p. 287). Thatcher was no less conscious of television's power, and a sympathetic 'World in Action' programme, made shortly before she challenged Heath, may have helped her gain the party leadership. As Prime Minister, and with professional advice, she made a great effort to cultivate her television skills and her image, and to develop a variety of roles: concerned mother, Iron Lady, simple housewife and world statesman. 'A medium that in any case tends to magnify personalities had been faced with a giant-sized one' (Cockerell 1988, p. 340).

Television's influence and ubiquity were illustrated again in the overthrow of Thatcher and the struggle to succeed her. Although the electorate was tiny − 372 Conservative Members of the Commons − the campaign was fought out not only in the corridors of Westminster but on national television, with extended interviews of the contenders and saturation coverage of each step in the contest.

Moulding the Image

Some Prime Ministers have had considerable success with the media. The Tory press, for example, treated Churchill with awe as a great statesman. Callaghan conveyed a strong, reliable image during his premiership – in Margach's words he 'got it right' (Margach 1978, p. 172). Others have struggled. Even before Suez, Eden was given a rough time by the press, especially by the Tory *Daily Telegraph*, which complained about indecisiveness and weak government, Heath was never at home either with the press or television. He regarded television 'with a combination of contempt and fear', and gave only three television interviews in his first year as Prime Minister, complaining of the 'inquisitorial' approach in which the interviewer's aim was 'to make clear to everybody that he is much cleverer than the politician' (Cockerell 1988, pp. 171–3). More common, however, is a mixture in which Prime Ministers, such as Macmillan, Wilson and Thatcher, have had periods of media success and failure. The probing television interviews in particular impose enormous pressures. Although Thatcher could often dominate these interviews she said of them: 'I hate them, I hate them, I hate them.' This is not surprising because so much rests on them and the premier's public image can change sharply in either direction depending on audience reaction. Macmillan, who at first had been billed as 'Supermac' partly from his confident handling of the media, later fell foul of the satire of the early 1960s when deference turned to iconoclasm, *Private Eye* gained fame or notoriety and the television show 'That Was the Week that Was – TW3' was built on irreverence for the establishment and ego trips for young media personalities like David Frost. Macmillan's image was transformed from an unflappable leader to an incompetent old bumbler.

Thatcher came to office fully conscious of the importance of promoting herself through the media, and from her first election campaign she used professional advice. As Prime Minister she continued on the same path. She agreed to appear on popular programmes like 'Jim'll Fix It', 'Yes, Minister', and the Jimmy Young radio programme. Six weeks before calling the 1983 election she guided the television cameras around No. 10, and she was increasingly dominant in her television appearances, overawing even seasoned interviewers like Robin Day. Nor was she above criticizing her own minister on television, as she did James Prior. However, television is a two-edged sword. The image of strength that she conveyed could easily slip into one of bossiness and bullying, so that some broadcasters spoke of the 'TBW' ('That bloody woman') factor. Thatcher was conscious of this and when asked after the Westland affair why she had not dismissed Michael Heseltine before he resigned from the Cabinet, she replied, 'Then you would have called me "bossy boots".'

Prime Ministers have therefore found the media a cruel master, and have sometimes given vent to their feelings. Eden, instead of ignoring his bad press, devoted a whole speech at Bradford in January 1956 to denouncing 'cantankerous newspapers'. Wilson, who had prided himself on his prowess with the media, finished a bitter, resentful man. He was convinced that most of the press and the BBC were against the Labour Party and himself in particular. 'One thing I find obsessional in Harold', wrote Crossman in May 1967, 'is his attitude to the press' (1976 vol. II, p. 349). In 1969 Wilson, already furious with the press for accusing Marcia Williams and her brother Anthony Field of shady land deals, blew his top when Noyes Thomas of the *News of the World* accurately forecast Mrs Williams' ennoblement. Wilson told Haines that he should not brief the lobby if Thomas were present, but Haines managed to avoid a confrontation.

Tension and Disputes

Although the disputes between Prime Ministers and the media have often involved clashes over personal images, other factors have also come into play. Television creates a public setting for the government's activities. Even when a Prime Minister has retained a strong individual image, television can produce a political climate that presents major problems for the government. That happened during the Labour government's troubles of 1978/9. Peter Jenkins has argued that the situation then was not nearly as bad as in 1974, when the lights went out during the 'three-day week', but in 1979 television focused public attention on the anarchy, pettiness and authoritarianism of some unions. 'In the Winter of Discontent', he concluded, 'television did for the class war what it had done for the war in Vietnam' (Jenkins 1987, p. 27). That raises the further issue of whether the media should be seen principally as observers or participants in the political scene. There can be no clear answer, for they are both, but friction arises when, for example, a newspaper prints a leaked government document or an investigative television programme attacks government policy.

There is also potential tension in times of crises or if issues of national security are at stake when the government believes that the media should support it. The BBC and ITV are obliged to exercise 'balance' but that is difficult to achieve in a 'political' dispute. During the Suez crisis Eden made a television broadcast (his 'man of peace' speech) and saw no case for the opposition's right of reply, because he was presenting himself as the national leader in a war situation and not a party leader. However, the BBC allowed Gaitskell to set out Labour's rejection of military action in a broadcast which was 'regarded by many as outstanding, by others as even treasonable' (Rhodes James 1986, p. 569). Later there were similar problems between Thatcher and the television authorities over coverage of the Falklands war and the continuing conflict in Northern Ireland. In these cases the issues were whether 'the enemy' (the Argentinians and the IRA) should be given a platform; and whether the government should be 'tried by television' for such incidents as the sinking of the Argentinian cruiser *Belgrano* and the shooting of IRA members in Gibraltar.

Wilson's premiership, which saw some of the fiercest quarrels, also exposed further tensions with the BBC. After good relations early on, disputes arose in which Wilson, having accused the BBC of bias, countered by using his powers of appointment to change senior BBC personnel, by refusing to appear on BBC programmes while appearing on ITV and by using the licence fee as a lever. Tony Benn explained: 'If there was anything he (Wilson) did not like on the BBC he would threaten them with not putting up the licence fee – it was as crude as that,' and Wilson acted, for example in 1966, when he refused to increase the £5 fee which had not been changed for years. In February 1970 Crossman noted that the Cabinet started with a half-hour lecture from Wilson on 'the battle he has been waging' with the BBC. Wilson claimed success in moving Lord Hill from Independent Television to be the BBC's Chairman, and in replacing Hugh Greene as Director General with Charles Curran. However, he went on to complain that the features department showed 'implacable enmity to the Government', and he compared his treatment unfavourably with that given to Heath (Crossman 1977, p. 813).

Like Wilson, Thatcher became involved in disputes with the BBC. When Stuart Young, the Chairman of the BBC, died in 1986 Thatcher appointed Marmaduke Hussey, the former managing director of Times Newspapers, who had a tough reputation and shared many of Thatcher's views. Norman Tebbit was reported to have said that the appointment was 'to make it bloody clear that things have to change: he is to get in there and sort it out – in days and not months' (Cockerell 1988, p. 312). There were also disputes over television coverage of controversial issues such as the Falklands war, the miners' strike and the US bombing of Libya from British bases. On such issues there was no meeting of minds between the Prime Minister and the broadcasters. Yet despite the feuds – on the reporting of crises and national security issues; the style of programmes in which premiers want to emphasize 'good news' while the media want to probe; the aggressive attitude of some interviewers and some Prime Ministers; and the personal images that are created – the relationship will never be broken, for each side needs the other.

5 Party and Elections

Political parties are the vehicles through which power is gained at elections and by which governments and Prime Ministers are sustained in parliament. Since 1945 Prime Ministers have been drawn from either the Labour or Conservative party. In the early post-war years there was a common assumption that Britain had settled into a two-party mould, but that came under serious challenge during the 1970s and 1980s as the Liberals and Social Democrats gained support and 'national' parties were active in Scotland and Wales. However, despite a decline in popular backing for the two main parties the mould held, and indeed by 1990 had regained much of its strength, so that the potential to form a government remained with the Conservative and Labour parties. Therefore, in this study, only the two parties which have provided Prime Ministers are considered.

Party leaders (including Prime Ministers) seek to knit their parties into effective organizations, conscious that the successes and failures of the party reflect directly on them as leaders, that their own strengths and weaknesses affect the party and that ultimately they are dependent on party support. Because parties are complex organizations, which operate in different settings (parliament, central and regional organizations and local constituencies) and make diverse demands on their leaders, a leader who excels in some aspects of the party role may be weak in others. For example, Wilson was a successful party leader on at least two counts: first, in welding together a difficult and diverse group of parliamentarians (he spoke of driving the party vehicle so fast that the occupants were too giddy to look out); second, in winning elections, which he did by making Labour a popular party not on the basis of socialist ideology but by pragmatic and opportunist leadership. Yet, he also encountered considerable difficulties inside the party, especially in his relations with the central organization (Transport House and the National Executive Council) and some of the unions. Equally, Heath had a mixed record. He came to the leadership after dominating the policy-making groups which the Conservatives set up after the 1964 election defeat, and as leader he continued to galvanize party thinking, but he proved a remote and inaccessible figure to MPs and party workers and had a poor election record.

Prime Ministers have the advantage over leaders of the opposition in that the exercise of power binds the party together — through patronage, parliamentary discipline and the pleasure of office compared with the frustration of opposition. However, on their side, opposition leaders can concentrate on party affairs, whereas Prime Ministers have mixed constituencies to satisfy and wider issues to face, and that can create tension between the demands of the party and those of government. In responding to these demands some Prime Ministers have emphasized their national rather than their party role. Seldon concluded that Churchill 'appeared to regard himself at times as a benign elder statesman, above party politics' (Hennessy and Seldon 1987, p. 73). In 1951 he unsuccessfully tried to persuade the Liberals to join his government, and told the Commons: 'What the House needs is a period of tolerant and constructive debating on the merits of the questions before us without nearly every speech on either side being distorted by the passions of one election or the preparations for another' (Gilbert 1988, p. 659). In October 1974 Heath issued a remarkable election message saying that in the current crisis the best hope was for a national coalition government involving all the parties, putting aside their differences and transcending party division (Young 1989, p. 90). When he failed to gain a majority, Heath unsuccessfully tried to negotiate a deal with the Liberals.

In contrast, Wilson and Thatcher saw their parties as the

foundation on which to build their national role. Wilson, who set out to make Labour the 'natural party of government', directed his efforts to holding the parliamentary party together and dismissed proposals for links with other parties. Thatcher, who also rejected the compromises required to make pacts with other parties, told the 1922 Committee in 1985: 'I am a more passionate Conservative now than on the day I stepped into No. 10 – and I was pretty passionate then' (Young 1989, p. 498). She saw the defeat of socialism, in the form of the Labour Party, as part of her political mission.

In terms of ideology, most leaders have been drawn from the mainstream of their parties: Attlee, Wilson and Callaghan for Labour; Eden, Heath, Home and Major for the Conservatives. However, there have been several exceptions. In the 1950s Labour was led by Hugh Gaitskell, a 'right winger', while in 1980 the party chose Michael Foot who was 'left of centre'. Although the Tory party had been less overt in its ideology and its internal divisions until the advent of Thatcher, in Churchill and Macmillan it had chosen two men who had been 'outsiders' in the 1930s. Even as Prime Ministers they did not always conform. Macmillan commented that Lord Salisbury had 'thought Disraeli not a good Tory. And I'm afraid he was right. Nor am I, if you mean by that a very orthodox Tory!' (Horne 1989, pp. 37–8). Margaret Thatcher, for all her commitment to the party, was an 'outsider' when she gained power and even in office retained a strong anti-establishment approach and her strong convictions created deep divisions within the party.

Party Differences

There are differences between the parties which affect the leaders. Labour has been more overtly ideological, more constitutionally minded, more prone to votes, and power is formally divided between different sections of the party thereby imposing constraints on the leader. It prides itself on being democratic. The Conservatives have relied more on precedence, style and unwritten norms. They have a 'top down' structure which gives the leader very obvious powers. However, Robert McKenzie argued in his classical study of political parties that differences between the party leaders were not as marked in practice as they appeared on paper, particularly when the parties were in power: Prime Ministers, whether Conservative or Labour, behaved in a similar fashion. As Attlee demonstrated, Labour leaders have accepted the monarch's invitation to form a government without reference back to the party, they have appointed their own Cabinets and they have not felt themselves strictly bound by conference resolutions. On their side, Tory leaders may have fewer formal limitations but they have been constrained by implicit norms and precedents and by consideration of party views and, in making appointments, by the established party hierarchy.

McKenzie's point was well made but it can be overstated for although the differences between the leadership of the two parties may have been exaggerated differences do exist. While the Tory leader has ultimate responsibility for party policy, the Labour leader shares that with the party conference and the National Executive Council (NEC). While the Conservatives have direct authority over party organization, choose the party chairman and in opposition appoint the Shadow Cabinet, Labour leaders enjoy none of these powers. No Labour leader could act as Thatcher did, when, dissatisfied at the performance of the party's Central Office in the 1987 elections, she changed those responsible by appointing Peter Brooke as party chairman with instructions to reorganize the office to her liking, but then moved Brooke on again in 1989 after an unsuccessful Euro election and appointed Kenneth Baker. A Conservative party chairman is expected to be 'a loyal supporter of the party leader' (Ingle 1987, p. 51).

Each party has its own ethos. The Conservatives have been compared with a family, which is hierarchical but in which there is interdependence, so that while the head of the family is respected and has the final say, he/she has to take account of the views of the rest (Norton in Minogue and Biddiss 1987, p. 23). The transmission of views within the party is two-way, but the emphasis tends to be downwards from the leader, and the leader has considerable discretion. This was so wide at the beginning of the period that Churchill while in opposition dispensed with a Shadow Cabinet and instead had two parallel committees: a 'consultative committee' which was at his personal invitation and the 'business committee' composed of chairmen of backbench committees. Much of that personal discretion persists. When Heath was made leader in 1965 he made major changes in party headquarters. Ten years later it was Thatcher's turn to root out Heath's most committed followers. 'It would have been remarkable', wrote Philip Norton, 'if Mrs Thatcher had not made the changes she did' (Minogue and Biddiss 1987, p. 27). However, the family analogy does not hold up on at least one important issue, for Conservative leaders are held to account, and the party has shown little loyalty to leaders who fail to win elections, or, in Thatcher's case, have lost popular support. There was an element of ruthlessness in the treatment of leaders like Home, Heath and Thatcher.

The problems of the Labour leaders have been different, for in their day-to-day activities they face chronic disputes about ideology and power within the party, and yet the party has been loyal to its leaders: it has never forced or elected one out of office. The Labour structure produces an interplay between the leader, the Parliamentary Labour Party (PLP), the National Executive Committee (NEC), the unions, the annual conference and the constituencies. Labour leaders have to deal with and try to gain support from 'a notoriously ungovernable body of comrades with a supremely hybrid constitution' (Morgan, *Contemporary Record* winter 1988). Often they succeed, particularly when they are Prime Ministers, but regular battles have to be fought. Wilson protested that 'The Prime Minister and the Cabinet cannot be instructed by the National Executive Committee or by the Conference,' but the fact that he made the statement shows the tension that exists (*The Times*, 15 October 1976). In Wilson's case he had good relations with the PLP, but neglected Transport House, and his relations with the NEC were said to be 'bad and forever worsening', and he often avoided NEC meetings and ignored its decisions (Haines 1977, p. 13).

There was an element of personal pique in Wilson's behaviour, but it was also his attempt to demonstrate that the parliamentary leadership was supreme. However, neither Wilson nor other Labour leaders have had it all their own way. There have been regular calls for tighter controls on them. Following the election defeat in 1979, Tony Benn complained that Labour Prime Ministers had too much power. He argued that tension inside the party was not created, as the media always claimed, by internal rifts – between 'left' and 'right', or the PLP and the party outside parliament, or unions and the NEC – instead the problem came 'from the tension that exists between the dominating power of the Party Leader, especially when he is Prime Minister, and the rest of the Labour movement'. Benn believed that unless the balance were redressed the party could never resolve its internal conflicts, and he went on to state that the leader should be more accountable, simply 'the last link in the process by which policies get implemented after they have been hammered out at conference and won approval at a general election'. Instead, he complained, Labour Prime Ministers had often treated the party outside parliament as just another pressure group. Benn further suggested that the PLP and not the Prime Minister should elect Cabinet ministers and exercise authority over business in the House in line with conference policy (Benn 1979).

The push and pull for power within Labour continued after the 1979 defeat. For a time it looked as though Benn's hopes would be fulfilled. New checks were placed on the leader: he was no longer chosen exclusively by the PLP but by an electoral college, he could be challenged for the leadership when Prime Minister as well as in opposition and he would be obliged to offer Cabinet posts to Shadow Cabinet members who were returned to parliament. However, Neil Kinnock, having been elected by the new method, proceeded to show how a leader with clear aims and tenacity could stamp his mark on the Labour Party even if he had to fight every inch of the way. Despite considerable internal opposition he purged the party of the Militant factor, changed the party's image and organization and persuaded it to abandon policies (such as unilateral nuclear disarmament) which had proved unpopular.

Conferences

Benn's emphasis on the Labour conference picks out another difference between the parties. Benn, and like-minded members, see the Labour conference as the source of policy and the party's final authority. No such claims have ever been made for the Conservative conference, which is more a rally than a policy forum. In the past the different demands this makes on leaders was reflected in their attendance. While Labour leaders have always attended the full conference — where they have often faced fierce criticism and lost votes (none more dramatic than Gaitskell's defeat in 1960 on nuclear policy) — Tory leaders used only to arrive for the final triumphant session. Heath changed that in 1965, and since then the leader has been present throughout the proceedings. More generally, the conferences have tended to move closer together, with Labour becoming more of a rally by the late 1980s and the Tory conference more policy-orientated. However, the atmosphere of the conferences remains different: the Conservative is that of a coffee ship full of lively gossipy chatter; the Labour is that of a pub on a Friday night with heated debates.

Both conferences exercise influence and create challenges for the leaders. Leaders of both parties pay great attention to their conference speeches, because they realize that failure to retain the support of the faithful exposes the whole party to division and media criticism. Douglas Hurd stated that: 'The most important speech in the year of the leader of the Conservative Party is made at the end of the Party Conference in October' (Hurd 1979, p. 76). However, while they pay respect to the conferences, neither Labour nor Tory leaders regard conference decisions as binding. That puts much greater pressure on Labour leaders, because of the views noted above, but no Labour leader has accepted that the conference has the final say. There were tremendous struggles in Wilson's time. In 1968, for example, the leadership was defeated 12 times, including a five-to-one defeat on the major issue of incomes policy, but Wilson refused to be bound. There were similar conflicts in the early 1970s, but the price Wilson paid was to lose control of part of the party organization. Life for the Tory leader is easier, for the conference does not claim the final say, but it is influential in that leaders try to adjust and respond to the issues raised and the mood of the gatherings. They try to keep in tune with the party faithful. For example, Rab Butler claimed that when the 1946 conference overwhelmingly demanded a revision of policy Churchill moved to meet it. However, Churchill, like other Tory leaders, certainly never felt bound by the conference. Later a colleague said of Heath that 'like Macmillan and R. A. Butler you always had the impression that Ted ... found some of the activists at Conference distasteful — backward-looking, complacent and reactionary,' and he did not share grass-root views on such issues as law and order, sentencing of criminals and immigration (Hennessy and Seldon 1987, p. 218).

In contrast, Richard Kelly has argued that one of Thatcher's strengths was that 'her opinions and prejudices are close in line with those who attend conference' (Kelly 1989, p. 156). Like other party leaders, she made a point of attending a number of party gatherings through the year in addition to the main conference. For example, in 1986, she appeared at the party's local government conference, the central council and the Conservative women's organization, so that when it came to the main conference in October she was well informed about party views, and able to respond to them, and in her case largely to share them. Yet there can be dangers for party leaders, and certainly one as committed as Thatcher, in listening too closely to the enthusiasms of party activists. That happened to her at the annual conference at Blackpool in 1987 when Gerry Malone dramatically urged the government to introduce the poll tax in England in one fell swoop. Fired by Malone's enthusiasm, the conference rose in support of 'the Big Bang', and for Thatcher, who was already inclined that way, the temptation was too great. She went with the conference tide instead of listening to the voices of caution from Cabinet colleagues like Nigel Lawson. It was a disastrous mistake.

Elections

Prime Ministers have a prominent party role in elections. First, they decide the date (within a maximum period of five years). Second, as party leaders, they are ultimately responsible for the party's election campaign and play a central part in it. Third, their leadership qualities (and those of opposition leader) are one of the issues at stake.

In deciding on the time of elections Prime Ministers often consult senior colleagues, but there is no set pattern. In 1959 Macmillan appears to have decided alone, but usually there is consultation with senior ministers, as in Attlee's case when in 1950 he consulted Morrison, Bevin, Bevan and Dalton, but sometimes wider consultation takes place. Before the 1970 election, for example, Wilson called a meeting of the inner Cabinet to discuss the election date. 'As a rule', wrote Denis Healey, 'a Prime Minister does not consult more than a handful of colleagues before picking the date; but on this occasion Harold wanted to be sure that the blame would be widely shared if he took the wrong decision' (Healey, 1989, p. 344).

Despite Wilson's hopes, the final decision, and therefore the responsibility, and with it the praise and blame, lies with the Prime Minister. Control of timing has clear advantages, for unpopular decisions can be delayed, opinion polls and economic statistics consulted and the economy massaged to give short-term benefits. Successful timing enhances a Prime Minister's reputation as Eden demonstrated when only nine days after gaining the premiership he called an election, and led the Conservatives back to power with an increased majority. It was a bold move. Eden's first instinct had been to delay for some months, but he changed his mind when he received strong advice that the economic situation would soon deteriorate. In February 1974 Wilson agreed to form a minority government, because, he said, 'the main thing is to get in there, form a Government and then control events and time the next election.' Thatcher also increased her hold on the party with the successful timing of the 1983 and 1987 elections.

Yet, while the advantages seem to be stacked on the government's side, the results of elections have been evenly balanced. Of the 13 held between 1945 and 1987 seven were won by the government and six by the opposition. Prime Ministers may mis-time elections or be forced into them when the government is weak and its policies in disarray, thereby underlining the point that elections are often lost by the government rather than won by the opposition. In 1951, Attlee, his tired government hanging onto a small majority, called an election which even Conservatives admitted was less to gain advantage than to clear the air. In 1974 Heath went to the country with the miners on strike and industry on a three-day working week. His instinct was to delay because he knew the problems would remain after the election, but senior party figures and the constituencies feared that continued uncertainty would lose support and favoured a 'Who rules?' campaign. Although Heath's cabinet was divided, 'a strange consensus emerged: not that an early election was necessarily desirable, but that for some reason it was inevitable' (King in Penniman 1975, p. 23). That election produced a wretched outcome for Heath. Labour gained more seats than the Tories but not an overall majority. Heath therefore tried to form a coalition with the Liberals, but failed, and was castigated by some critics for trying to hold onto power and by others for losing the election and flirting with the Liberals. Equally strong were the criticisms heaped on Callaghan after the 1979 election. To the surprise of many of his followers, but supported by senior colleagues, Callaghan decided not to call an election in autumn 1978 when the economy was in reasonable shape, Labour was ahead in the polls and the pact with the Liberals was still holding. Callaghan delayed because he assumed he needed more time to establish himself, that the Liberals would hold firm and the unions would continue to support the government. All those assumptions were wrong, and Callaghan was forced into an election, not from choice, but when the government was defeated in the Commons, after being undermined by the unions during 'the winter of discontent'. It was a disastrous election for Labour.

Prime Ministers play prominent parts in the election campaigns. Although the campaigns have changed greatly between 1945 and 1987 they are always intense and stressful. As well as their ultimate responsibility for the party machine, for the election manifesto and the broad strategy to be pursued, Prime Ministers also have to decide on their personal role. Campaigns, therefore, test them both as public figures and as organizers. In the early years party organization was less professional. The leaders prepared a general message, left the detailed arrangements to others and made contact with the electorate through national tours, the press and a few radio broadcasts. The tours could be physically and mentally exhausting. In 1950, for example, Attlee spoke in seven towns on each day during an eight-day tour. Although that style of electioneering disappeared, later campaigns were no less taxing. By the 1980s the leaders were immersed in the organization, surrounded by professional advisers and advertising agents, and from their London base they made quick forays into the rest of the country. Most striking of all, however, was the emphasis on television, with its interviews, party political broadcasts, 'picture opportunities' and news 'sound bites'.

Despite the changes the personalities of the leaders have always played a part in elections. The contrast has never been greater than when Attlee, the master of understatement, and Churchill, the conquering hero, went electioneering. Churchill set out 'to meet the people' surrounded by a cavalcade of supporters and cars. Attlee's approach was more modest. 'While his wife drives', wrote the *Daily Mirror*, 'Mr Attlee puts on his glasses, rests on a brown and green folk-weave cushion, and does the crossword puzzles .... If their car is held up at a level crossing Mrs Attlee gets out her knitting – a pair of grey socks' (Harris 1982, p. 491). Personality became even more prominent with the advent of television. Television made a faltering start in the 1955 election when Eden made a broadcast, but from 1959 it came to play a central part in campaigns. In television news during the 1970 campaign 56 per cent of total Labour coverage was given to Wilson and 60 per cent of Conservative to Heath, and by 1987 76 per cent of broadcast references to speeches were taken from the party leaders. The leaders' television performances could therefore make or break the campaign, and the challenge of face-to-face confrontation changed from hecklers at a public meeting to professional interviewers, who adopted increasingly aggressive and inquisitorial approaches. Alec Douglas-Home tried to resist the change. In

1964 he set out on an old-fashioned tour, but, ironically, it is best remembered for television pictures of him being heckled in Birmingham. After that all leaders recognized that television had to be the major component in their campaigns.

The personal and organizational aspects of campaigning were illustrated in Wilson's handling of the 1966 election when he emphasized his personal role as leader at the expense of the party machine. After winning a narrow victory in 1964, Wilson showed great strategic skill in 1966 by underlining the government's stability and confidence, in refusing to make wild promises, personally remaining aloof until near the end of the campaign, limiting his television appearances, delegating some press conferences to Callaghan and sending George Brown out of trouble on a national tour. After the 1966 victory even his critics within the party trusted his expertise in campaigning and saw him as a major election asset. Yet Wilson had relied on his personal efforts and his own staff rather than the party organization, and a gulf grew between him and Transport House. His campaign was based on the belief that political circumstances and his own leadership would carry the day, and 'Transport House advice probably mattered much less than the suggestions from his personal entourage in 10 Downing Street and from one or two of his senior colleagues' (Butler and Pinto-Duschinsky 1971, p. 145). In contrast, Heath, who constantly trailed Wilson as a leader in the opinion polls, was in a weaker personal position. After losing the 1966 election, and with less personal pull, he concentrated on overhauling the party machine. He replaced du Cann as Chairman with Anthony Barber, and established policy groups in which he personally took an active interest.

Heath's emphasis on organization may have paid off, for the Conservatives won the 1970 election, and on the whole the Conservative machinery has been the more efficient, although Labour has improved under Neil Kinnock. However, as the electoral tension mounts there can be confusion and conflict even among the Tories, as in 1987, when two separate plots ran through the party's campaign: one was the public fight against Labour and the Alliance; the other was the internal struggle between Thatcher and Norman Tebbit, the Party

Chairman. Thatcher, who suspected that Tebbit was trying to diminish her part in the campaign and build his own power base, retaliated by setting up an alternative organization under David Young and appointing another advertising agency.

Although an election is not a presidential contest, the premiership is at stake. It is impossible to say precisely how important that is in the overall pattern of voting, and it probably varies between elections, but electors know that they are voting for a Prime Minister and a government as well as a local candidate. In that respect there can be a danger of placing too much reliance on the leader, as the Conservatives discovered in 1945 when they concentrated on 'selling' Churchill, the great war leader whose personality far outshone Attlee's. In contrast Labour offered policies and a team approach and won. However, party leadership is a factor and it has become more important with television's concentration on personalities. A negative example helps to underline the point. In 1983 the Labour Party not only issued a manifesto which one supporter described as 'the longest suicide note in history', but in Michael Foot they had a leader who, in opinion poll after opinion poll, lagged far behind Thatcher, was poor on television and lacked the qualities the electorate was looking for in a Prime Minister. Thatcher outshone him on television and ran a much more effective campaign. It would be perverse to ignore this as one of the factors that helped the Conservatives. However, Thatcher's earlier experience also demonstrated that the leadership is only one issue for the electors. In 1979 she consistently trailed Callaghan in opinion polls as a potential Prime Minister and yet she won the election easily because the voters rejected the Labour government's record.

6 Parliament

The House of Commons is the arena in which Prime Ministers are judged by fellow politicians. In the small intense world of Westminster they are scrutinized and tested by their own side as well as by the opposition. A Prime Minister's hold on the House is crucial to his/her hold on power. In 1953, Churchill, following his severe illness, concluded: 'I must be sure that I can master the House of Commons. I'm not worried about anything else, but if I can't master the House I must not go on' (Gilbert 1988, p. 866). Macmillan, who claimed that he was less worried about losing by-elections than control in parliament, said that 'If you can once impress upon the House of Commons that the government is strong and the Prime Minister is in control ... then gradually it begins to go out into the country .... Then gradually the Press begin to show a certain surprise at the success of the Government' (Horne 1989, p. 20). Although in more recent times Prime Ministers have spent less time in the House and made fewer contributions, the need for parliamentary support is still crucial.

As Macmillan had recognized, image as well as substance is important in parliament. Each Prime Minister tries to convey the message that the government is on top of its job and can counter the wiles of the opposition. In achieving those ends Prime Ministers have the advantages of being clothed in the robes of authority and backed both by the machinery of government and the majority party. Leaders, like Attlee and Home, who were not effective in opposition, performed well as Prime Ministers. In 1945 the Tories believed that in Churchill they had a parliamentary champion who would dominate Attlee and undermine the government. However, Attlee held his own against Churchill, like a 'small and nimble toreador teasing and infuriating his magnificent opponent with his sudden barbs' (Burridge 1985, p. 197). Equally unfounded were Tory fears that Home would not be able to stand up to Wilson, a renowned opposition leader. Yet at other times Prime Ministers have been in trouble in the House during crises and/or when they were losing their grip. Eden had a torrid time during Suez and sometimes wilted under parliamentary pressure. Ian Waller wrote of an 'inept and inconclusive' performance in which at one stage he had to be rescued by the Speaker. 'The Government won the vote, but Sir Anthony suffered a blow to his prestige that was clearly reflected in the silent, devastated ranks on the Conservative benches behind him' (McKenzie 1963, p. 584). Towards the end of his career Macmillan also showed signs of losing his parliamentary touch, especially during the Profumo affair, and that may have been a factor in influencing his decision to retire. In January 1986, during the Westland helicopter affair, Thatcher left Downing Street for the Commons, saying, 'I may not be Prime Minister by six o'clock tonight' (Young 1989, p. 454). That dramatic outburst was based on her concern that the opposition would exploit divisions in the Tory ranks to overthrow the government. In the event Kinnock failed to seize his opportunity and the Conservatives rallied behind the Prime Minister.

The Premiers' Contributions

Dunleavy, Jones and O'Leary have assessed the contributions of premiers in the Commons between 1868 and 1987 in four ways: answering questions, making ministerial statements, delivering speeches and minor interventions (e.g. impromptu responses to MPs' speeches). Based on the number of parliamentary days between contributions they concluded that 1940 (when Churchill became wartime Prime Minister) was a dividing line. There were variations but on the whole premiers who served before 1940 were 'multi-faceted' parliamentarians and contributed more than those who followed. In the post-1945 period there was little to choose between Prime Ministers in answering parliamentary questions, but in all other respects there were differences which became marked from 1976 when the Prime Minister's contributions declined sharply, first with Callaghan and even more with Thatcher. For example, in terms of speeches Eden was the most regular performer, averaging a speech every 15 days whereas Thatcher averaged 45. An even greater difference came in impromptu contributions. While other premiers' interventions averaged between 10 and 18 days Callaghan's was 33 and Thatcher's 100. In three parliamentary sessions 1985/6, 1986/7 and 1987/8 (508 days in all) Thatcher made no debating interventions.

The three authors advanced a number of possible explanations

Table 6.1 Frequency of parliamentary questions, speeches and interventions (based on number of parliamentary days)

	Question time	Speeches	Debating interventions
Attlee	Every 2.0 days	Every 28 days	Every 13 days
Churchill	Every 2.6 days	Every 20 days	Every 9 days
(including wartime)			
Eden	Every 3.5 days	Every 15 days	Every 10 days
Macmillan	Every 3.0 days	Every 26 days	Every 17 days
Home	Every 2.8 days	Every 26 days	Every 10 days
Wilson	Every 2.3 days	Every 25 days	Every 13 days
Heath	Every 2.8 days	Every 28 days	Every 10 days
Callaghan	Every 2.8 days	Every 27 days	Every 33 days
Thatcher	Every 2.8 days	Every 45 days	Every 100 days

Source: P. Dunleavy, G. W. Jones and O'Leary, *Public Administration* spring 1990.

for Thatcher's 'minimalist parliamentary activity': that she preferred running the executive to presiding in parliament; that she only felt comfortable in scripted situations; that she was uneasy in the predominantly male atmosphere of the Commons. They noted that 'many of her statements seem to express a perception of the Commons as a distinctly hostile environment, rather than the friendly male debating club which some previous premiers enjoyed dominating' (*Public Administration* spring 1990, p. 135). They might have added a further possibility – that Thatcher avoided unrehearsed situations because the degree of bitterness in the House had risen sharply as she set out to break the post-war consensus in her crusade against socialism. Yet ironically one of the abiding memories of Thatcher's premiership is her final speech as Prime Minister. The speech came on a motion of no confidence in the government which the opposition had put down while Thatcher was still embroiled in the leadership contest with Heseltine. By the time she came to speak she had already announced her withdrawal from the next stage of the contest. Far from wilting under the pressure she gave a brilliant performance, and to add to the irony its impact was all the greater because it was seen on television screens around the country, whereas she had always opposed televising parliament.

The reduction in Prime Ministerial activity might be taken as an indication of a decrease in the importance of parliament. That would be a mistake. Parliament is not a policy-making body, but it is the place where ministers are held accountable for government policies, where political reputations are made and lost, and where the concerns of the nation are publicly exposed. These factors continued to be as important for Callaghan and Thatcher as they had been for Churchill and Macmillan. Even if Thatcher's direct contributions were mainly confined to question time, the questions that were asked and the effectiveness with which she handled them had a direct impact on her and her government. Although she, like other Prime Ministers, often dominated parliamentary opponents, in times of trouble her touch was less secure, for example during conflicts over nurses' pay, policy towards the EEC and the poll tax. Each situation compounds itself. When a government is riding high a Prime Minister can enter the House with confidence, but when it is in trouble he/she will face a fierce interrogation knowing that they and the government are on trial.

In such circumstances even the most dominant of parliamentarians have to work for their success. Macmillan and Wilson took great pains to improve their skills and style, and the Commons was the one forum for which Wilson always wrote his speeches. Despite such preparation Prime Ministers are under great pressure. All have worked hard for question times, and a major task of one of the private secretaries in No. 10 is preparation for these sessions. Even those who have handled questions well (such as Wilson and Thatcher) found them ordeals. Wilson was said to hate them and to be nervous before entering the House. Thatcher, who was equally nervous, prepared meticulously and ate little before the ordeal, but at her best she was able to use question time as a platform to project herself and her government. 'This fifteen minute session is regarded as of crucial importance, partly because she permits any topic at all to be raised. She thinks that Questions are her hotline to the British people' (Madgwick 1984, p. 41).

Leaders and Backbenchers

In their relations with party backbenchers Prime Ministers have both formal and informal links. The formal include the Whips' Office, which keeps the Prime Minister in touch with party views and rallies support for government policies, and is so important that the Chief Whip has enjoyed a permanent Cabinet seat since Heath's premiership. Another link comes through backbench organizations − for Labour the PLP, and for Conservatives the 1922 Committee (named after a meeting at the Carlton Club in 1922 when backbenchers voted against the leader Austen Chamberlain). Normally relations between Prime Ministers and the chairmen of the backbench groups are amicable, but not always. In 1974 one sign of disquiet among Tory MPs with Heath's leadership was the election of Edward du Cann as chairman of the 1922 Committee, for despite du

Cann's abilities, Heath had earlier dismissed him as Party Chairman and had not offered him a ministerial post.

The tone of meetings between premiers and backbenchers depends on the prevailing political climate. Usually they are supportive or are routine exchanges of views and information, but if the government is in difficulties they can be tense, and the outcome can determine whether the government is seen to be in charge or in trouble. Wilson's contrasting experiences were recorded by Barbara Castle and Richard Crossman who were members of his Cabinet. Castle wrote of an end-of-term meeting in July 1974 when Wilson gave a crowded meeting a catalogue of the government's recent achievements. Castle found it 'pedestrian' but it was well received by the PLP. There was less enthusiasm in March of the following year when Wilson made a low-key speech 'running through the Manifesto shopping list like a bored housewife at the grocer's' (Castle 1980, pp. 160 and 341). Wilson faced some mild criticism at that meeting, but it was as nothing compared with the barrage he had faced in 1969 when he had tried to introduce a new Industrial Relations Act ('In Place of Strife'). Crossman wrote of Wilson coming under fierce attack from such powerful speakers as Michael Foot and Eric Heffer, backed by the vast majority of the PLP. In response Wilson was 'a complete flop', making 'a disastrous wind-up, a bumbling, fumbling, argumentative reply, devastating in its failure'. For Wilson it was, in Crossman's view, a disastrous experience after which his authority in the PLP sank to a new low (Crossman 1977, pp. 444−5).

The talents and inclinations of Prime Ministers have varied greatly in their informal relations with Members of Parliament. Some, like Churchill and Callaghan, made easy contact in the Commons' bars, smoking room and tea room, but others, like Eden and Heath, were unclubbable and notoriously poor at relaxing with backbenchers or indeed even knowing who they were. Macmillan and Thatcher, who followed Eden and Heath respectively, absorbed the lesson and in their early days as Prime Minister went out of their way to encourage contact and be seen in the Commons' social areas. However, for all Prime Ministers time and generation pose problems. The longer they stay in office, consumed with the affairs of state and often drawn from an older generation than many of their followers, the more difficult it becomes for them to avoid remoteness from their backbenchers and even ministerial colleagues. Although in her early days Thatcher had been seen regularly in the Commons' tea room she lost the habit and it was an unusual event when she reappeared in November 1990, as she sought support in her campaign against Heseltine. By then none of her original Cabinet colleagues was still in office.

Prime Ministers anticipate backbench voting support even if some members have doubts over government policies. Seldom are Prime Ministers disappointed, for only in extreme circumstances would backbenchers think of endangering the party's hold on power by staging a full-scale revolt. However, there has been a change in relationships. In the early post-war years party leaders tended to view backbenchers as voting 'cannon fodder'. Wilson rammed home the point with his 'dog licence' speech, when he warned Labour MPs who had disobeyed the whips that if they bit once more they were in danger of having their licences withdrawn. Discipline was so tight that between 1950 and 1959 97 per cent of the divisions saw complete party cohesion. However, since the early 1970s there has been a change. Philip Norton has argued that this has increased the effectiveness of parliament because leaders have had to pay more attention to MPs. Norton associated the change with Heath's 'Olympian style of leadership' in which backbenchers were expected to follow obediently the shifts of government policies while Heath made no effort to build effective links with them. They reacted against this and Heath's government was defeated six times. The change outlived Heath, so that the minority Labour administrations which followed suffered many defeats, and MPs retained some of their independence under Thatcher, forcing her to head off dissension by making concessions, as, for example, on students' loans, selling off parts of British Leyland to Americans and the poll tax (Norton, *Contemporary Record* autumn 1988). Prime Ministers are therefore more prepared now to respond to backbench views and to tolerate greater freedom for MPs, but they do so on the clear understanding that the main duty of backbenchers is to sustain them and their government.

7 The Cabinet

The Cabinet is the central executive body of government: coordinating activity, approving developments, settling departmental disputes and keeping senior ministers informed of the overall thrust of policy. The Cabinet's major figure is the Prime Minister, who chooses and dismisses its members, chairs the meetings, agrees the agenda and decides on the composition and tasks of its committees. The Cabinet can therefore be seen as a source of power for Prime Ministers, but also as a constraint upon them in that they have to act within the framework of a group composed of powerful ministers.

The conventional picture of 'Cabinet government' is one in which the Cabinet as a body, led by the Prime Minister, directs and oversees the government's activities. But provisos have to be made. First, the scale and nature of government activity means that not only the Prime Minister but the Cabinet cannot oversee it all. Second, while most major policies pass through Cabinet there are exceptions: for example, Prime Ministers have consciously kept out of Cabinet key decisions about atomic and nuclear weapons. Third, although the Cabinet performs a range of tasks it does not necessarily perform them all effectively at the same time. There is variation according to the circumstances of the day and the Prime Minister's approach. Fourth, all premiers put distinctive stamps on their Cabinets. Some premiers are more assertive than others and they use the Cabinet in different ways, both in the conduct of business and its role within the government. Fifth, while the Cabinet sometimes operates as a single body, frequently Prime Ministers will work with individual ministers or small groups, and sometimes form an 'inner Cabinet'. Sixth, although Prime Ministers rely heavily on Cabinet colleagues, they also turn for support and advice elsewhere, and therefore the Cabinet is best seen as part of a central executive and not its sole body (see chapter 8). Finally the Cabinet is often best understood not as a single body but a network of committees of which the full Cabinet is the coordinating body. However, despite all these provisos, the Cabinet does play a major part in government, and on occasions flexes its corporate muscle, sometimes against the Prime Minister.

Hiring and Firing

Prime Ministers appoint and dismiss Cabinet members and allocate their portfolios. This has given them great power, for all politicians are ambitious for office. According to Aneurin Bevan 'There are only two ways of getting into the cabinet: to crawl up the staircase of preferment on your belly', or ' to kick them in the teeth' (Hennessy 1986, p. 94). The prospect of office has converted most Members of Parliament into 'staircase' men. When a recalcitrant figure remains, the Prime Minister has to decide whether to buy him off with ministerial office (as Wilson and Callaghan did with Tony Benn) or to send him into the wilderness (as Heath did with Enoch Powell and Thatcher with Heath). Neither solution is completely satisfactory for 'the rebel' is unlikely to prove a loyal minister but if he remains outside he may be a thorn in the government's flesh.

In making their decisions Prime Ministers have sometimes consulted their senior colleagues including the Chief Whip, and even senior civil servants, as Churchill did with Norman Brook the Cabinet secretary, but Prime Ministers have not had unfettered choice. They have to select from within parliament and mainly the Commons. They have to take account of party interests, to reward most of the leading figures and to ensure the future by bringing in new blood. Sometimes disappointed rivals have had to be appeased, as in 1957 and 1976 when Macmillan and Callaghan respectively asked Butler and Foot what Cabinet post they wanted, and in 1990 when Major brought Heseltine into the government for the sake of party unity. Political circumstances can strengthen or weaken the Prime Minister's position. When Home came to office in 1963 he was in a weak position because of the party's divisive leadership struggle and because he inherited a powerful, experienced and partly dissatisfied Cabinet. In the following year Wilson's situation was very different. He had won an election, he had no rival for the leadership and most of his colleagues had no Cabinet experience. In contrast, when Thatcher gained the premiership most Tory leaders were experienced 'Heath men' and she formed a Cabinet many of whose members did not share her views.

Although these constraints have operated, so far all Prime Ministers, irrespective of party, have had personal discretion in Cabinet appointments, but a limitation could operate in future for Labour leaders. In the past the PLP when in opposition has elected the 'Shadow Cabinet' but in power Labour Prime Ministers had enjoyed full discretion. However, since 1981 the standing orders of the PLP require an incoming Labour Prime Minister to include in his Cabinet all members of the Shadow Cabinet who are returned to parliament. As Labour has been in opposition since then, the order has not been put into operation and its full consequences are unclear.

The allocation of portfolios has offered Prime Ministers further discretion. For example, Macmillan, eager to gain admission to the EEC, ensured that pro-Europeans were in crucial posts: Heath, as Privy Seal, was given responsibility for the negotiations, while Christopher Soames and Duncan Sandys were given Agriculture and Commonwealth Relations to counter the adverse reactions anticipated from these areas. As noted above, in 1979 when Thatcher came to power her position was fragile because most of her first Cabinet were 'Heath men'. She countered this by ensuring that economic management was in the hands of her supporters and over the years she weeded out or marginalized those who were not 'one of us'.

However, again there are constraints. Leading party figures

not only want to be in the Cabinet, they want major posts. Both Attlee and Wilson made poor appointments to the Foreign Office because of this. Attlee later admitted that: 'It was a bad mistake allowing Herbert (Morrison) to be Foreign Secretary. I didn't know he knew so little. I had no idea he was so ignorant' (Shlaim 1977, p. 79). In Wilson's case he decided to move George Brown to the Foreign Office to avoid a party split. According to Marcia Williams, the reasons were negative: 'Partly because of his (Brown's) announced desire to resign, and partly because he felt he no longer carried authority in the Department of Economic Affairs' (Williams 1972, p. 151). Other powerful ministers have laid down terms. In 1955 Eden wanted to move his two most senior colleagues: Macmillan from the Foreign Office to the Treasury where he would replace Butler who would become Leader of the House. Eden's main motive was to regain personal control of foreign policy and so he gave way when Macmillan, already with an eye on the succession, said he would only move if Butler did not retain the title 'Deputy Prime Minister'. Eden weakly agreed, although he insisted that Bulter continued to chair Cabinet meetings in his absence. In other circumstances a minister may be difficult to move because he is entrenched in a post, or because the party might react against it or it might attract adverse publicity.

A Prime Minister may allocate portfolios because of the ministers' expertise, for example when Eden and Home were given the Foreign Office, and Cripps and Lawson were made Chancellors of the Exchequer. Yet, there are many exceptions to this, even in the most senior posts. Selwyn Lloyd and John Major were made Foreign Secretaries (albeit for only three months in Major's case) although they had shown little interest in foreign affairs. Another factor is the direction the Prime Minister wants the government to take. Churchill and Wilson, who both wanted to avoid confrontation with the trades unions, appointed ministers in charge of labour relations who were sympathetic to the unions (Walter Monckton and Michael Foot). 'When', said Wilson, 'I told the union leaders Michael Foot was Secretary of State for Employment, Jack Jones had a broad grin on his face' (Holmes 1985, p. 1). Thatcher allocated portfolios to ensure that her Cabinet critics were moved to the periphery, notably James Prior to Northern Ireland and Peter Walker to the Welsh Office. Prime Ministers are also influenced by their personal interests. When they want an active role they either choose a minister who shares their views and with whom they can work closely, as Thatcher did when she made Geoffrey Howe Chancellor, or a compliant figure like Selwyn Lloyd, who served Eden and Macmillan.

Prime Ministers dismiss as well as appoint. It is a job which most of them hate, because of the tension and animosity it creates and because if they handle it badly it weakens the government. However, being a 'good butcher' is one of the character-istics of a strong Prime Minister. Crossman said he would look across the table at Wilson and realize that like Henry VIII the Prime Minister had the power to cut off his (political) head. However, Wilson (despite Crossman's comment) was not a good butcher. He disliked confrontation, and gave a high priority to party unity which could be undermined by dismissals. In contrast Attlee was renowned for his clinical, crisp approach. One junior minister, summoned by Attlee, came anticipating congratulations, only to be told, 'I want your job.' When the astonished minister asked why, Attlee said, 'Afraid you're not up to it,' and that was that (Harris 1982, p. 407). In contrast, Churchill, although complaining about colleagues, was reluctant to remove them and was criticized for holding on to old friends.

With some changes Prime Ministers have no choice: for example, Iain Macleod's early death obliged Heath to find a new Chancellor. Resignations by Cabinet ministers can be awkward. Most are for personal reasons or ill health, which may be unwelcome to the Prime Minister but do not cause great problems. However, resignations for other reasons are much more difficult, because they may expose divisions or in-competence within the government or may be a form of criticism of its leader. Some resignations have come after policy clashes, for example, when Bevan and Wilson left Attlee's cabinet over defence expenditure, and when in Macmillan's government Salisbury resigned over colonial policy and Thorneycroft over the economy. However, some of the most dramatic departures have been about the way the government is run. When George Brown resigned from Wilson's Cabinet in 1968 he complained that the Prime Minister was introducing presidential government, taking decisions over the heads of ministers and giving too much power to advisers outside the Cabinet. He concluded that effective cooperation was impossible (Brown 1971, pp. 169–74). In 1986 Michael Heseltine resigned by walking out of Thatcher's Cabinet during the Westland helicopter affair. He opposed the decision that was taken, but his main complaint was the Prime Minister's disregard for Cabinet government and her authoritarian style. He spoke of 'the breakdown of constitutional government'.

The experience of Thatcher's Cabinets underlines the mixed pattern. By the time she lost office in November 1990 13 Cabinet ministers had resigned in her 11 years, several in the last two years. There were a variety of reasons behind these decisions: Carrington (1982) went after public criticism of his handling of the Falklands crisis; Keith Joseph (1986) decided that he had served long enough in parliament; Lord Whitelaw (1988) went from ill health; George Younger (1989) to pursue a business career; Norman Fowler (1990) and Peter Walker (1990) to give more time to their private lives; Nicholas Ridley (1990) after his outrageous statements about the Germans had made his position untenable; and Jim Prior (1984), Michael Heseltine (1986), Nigel Lawson (1989) and Geoffrey Howe (1990) over policy differences. It was the last group, those who resigned after direct clashes, which were most dangerous for the Prime Minister, and it was Howe's resignation which led to Thatcher's fall.

Reshuffles

Cabinets require regular maintenance and repair. The process provides a further test for Prime Ministers, because changing the team can sometimes be more difficult than the initial selection. At the beginning of an administration the Prime Minister is often in a powerful position, especially following a successful election and before senior colleagues are entrenched. The test comes with 'the reshuffle', when the Prime Minister chooses to reorganize the Cabinet, usually to the accompaniment of intense party and media speculation. There is no set pattern, for each Prime Minister decides when and how often reshuffles take place. For example, a comparison shows that the Labour government of 1964/70 was more volatile than that of 1974/9, with 15 sets of changes in the first period and only eight in the second. Part of the explanation is that in the first period Wilson was a Prime Minister in a hurry, whereas in the second he and his successor, Callaghan, saw themselves as elder statesmen.

The aim of reshuffles is to give fresh life to the government, but if they happen often or are badly handled they can antagonize the party and be interpreted as a sign of weakness, not strength. Reshuffles vary greatly in their scope, from minor adjustments to major surgery, but all require a delicate touch. Crossman, for instance, complained that the constant changes of the first Wilson period undermined the power of ministers in relation to their civil servants. Prime Ministers have also been criticized for doing too little as well as too much. Eden was accused of indecision because he made few changes after succeeding Churchill. 'Anthony never built a Cabinet in his own mould,' said a colleague, 'He inherited one, and then tinkered with it' (Rhodes James 1986, p. 405). Callaghan was more positive when he followed Wilson. He kept many of the Cabinet's leading figures, but stamped his authority by removing Barbara Castle and William Ross, and when Tony Crosland, the Foreign Secretary, died, Callaghan decided to replace him with David Owen: 'It would do the government no harm', he wrote, 'if I surprised the press and others ... by bringing in someone fresh and young,' and it would strengthen 'the group of younger cabinet ministers who would be restless, with new ideas and prevent a feeling of staleness' (Callaghan, 1987, p. 448).

In 1990, although Major did not make many changes in the Cabinet he inherited from Thatcher, he put his stamp upon it by promoting his lieutenant Norman Lamont to be Chancellor of the Exchequer, giving Malcolm Rifkind Transport in place of Cecil Parkinson, and, most striking of all, by giving a Cabinet seat to Michael Heseltine.

A smooth reshuffle enhances the Prime Minister's reputation, whereas a rough one damages it. Thatcher had contrasting experiences. In 1988 she surprised everybody (and nonplussed the opposition) by announcing a reshuffle in July, instead of the usual September. She thereby avoided media and party speculation, and, as the changes were relatively small and the government was riding high in the opinion polls, she received general acclaim. 1989 was very different. This time media speculation was intense as a July reshuffle was anticipated, and when it came there was a major furore not only because the changes were greater than expected, but because they were badly handled. No one, including the ministers, anticipated that Thatcher would touch her three most senior colleagues: Howe (Foreign Secretary), Lawson (Treasury) and Hurd (Home Office). They were wrong. She decided, without warning or consultation, to remove Howe from the FCO. He was 'dumb-struck' and resentful. When, in the ensuring difficult discussions, Howe hesitated over accepting Leadership of the Commons, she offered him the Home Office, without consulting Hurd. Eventually Howe accepted Leadership of the House and Deputy Prime Minister (although Thatcher's press secretary made clear that 'Deputy' carried little weight) and she arranged for Howe the use of a country house previously allocated to Lawson, again without consultation. This incompetent piece of mangement antagonized three senior colleagues, raised an outcry in the party and the media about the way she had treated faithful colleagues and intensified her dictatorial image.

Macmillan had had an even more damaging experience in July 1962 − the 'night of the long knives'. His 'unflappable' reputation disintegrated as he dismissed a third of his Cabinet at one stroke. Again it was the way things were done that rebounded on him − the sense of unfairness, the secretiveness, the dictatorial style and the hint of panic. Macmillan might claim that he was bringing in new life and drive to a government that had lost its sparkle, for the average age of those who left was 60 and those who entered 49, but because of inept handling all the dismissed ministers gained sympathy, not least Selwyn Lloyd who had served Macmillan faithfully as Foreign Secretary and Chancellor. Whatever his intention, Macmillan looked like a man determined to hold on to power at the expense of his colleagues. A bitter Lloyd wrote of Macmillan's 'utter ruthlessness, and his determination to retain power by the sacrifice of even his closest friends' (Thorpe 1989, p. 354). Another of those dismissed, Lord Kilmuir, concluded: 'He was extremely alarmed about his own position and was determined to eliminate any risk for himself by a massive change of government' (Hennessy 1986 p. 61).

The Cabinet at Work

The personalities, skills and styles of Prime Ministers influence the way in which Cabinet business is conducted, the atmosphere within it and the Cabinet's role in the machinery of government. A wartime minister who served under Attlee and Churchill recalled, 'When Attlee takes the chair, Cabinet meetings are businesslike and efficient; we keep to the agenda, make decisions, and get away in reasonable time. When Churchill presides nothing is decided; we listen enthralled and go home, many hours later, feeling we have been present at an historic occasion' (Margach 1981, p. 15). What the minister failed to add was that the two leaders were using the Cabinet in different ways. Attlee wanted decisions — a clearing house for government business — whereas Churchill wanted a sounding board for broad sweeps of policy.

The different uses of the Cabinet persisted in post-war years. Attlee often acted more like an umpire than a team leader, which could not be said of either Heath or Thatcher. Heath was managerially minded, eager to lead an efficient team, 'a problem solver first, and ideologue only a distant second' (Hennessy 1986, p. 74). Thatcher, unlike most Prime Ministers, often started Cabinet discussions by outlining her position based on her strong convictions and then, if necessary, fighting for it against her colleagues. In the early days, before she had a like-minded team, this led to bitter disputes which she sometimes extended into the public arena by acting as a critic of her own administration.

The Prime Minister decides when the Cabinet meets, approves its agenda, chairs the meetings, summarizes the discussion and decides whether an issue will be referred to one of the Cabinet's committees. Even apparently mundane decisions like seating arrangements can have significance. During Macmillan's premiership Home entered the Cabinet room to find that places had been changed. When he asked the secretary if there had been a 'shuffle', he was told: 'Oh no, it's nothing like that. The Prime Minister cannot stand Enoch Powell's steely and accusing eyes looking him across the table any more, and I've had to move him down the side.' Later, James Prior explained how Heath tried to isolate Thatcher. 'She sat in cabinet', he said, 'on his (Heath's) right side, carefully hidden by the Secretary of the cabinet, who was always leaning foward to take notes. It was the most difficult place for anyone to catch the Prime Minister's eye, and I am sure that she was placed there deliberately' (Hennessy 1986, pp. 64 and 117).

More obviously Prime Ministers can influence and even control the flow of Cabinet business through the agenda. On occasions this has enabled them to avoid topics either because they do not trust some of their colleagues to keep a confidence (for example on nuclear issues) or because they believe they can gain their way by avoiding debate (as Wilson did with devaluation and Eden with the European Community). On a more positive note, Prime Ministers are in the best position to coordinate the work of the government through the Cabinet. Most Cabinet ministers are primarily concerned with their own departments, whereas the Prime Minister is in a position to see the total picture − to preserve and project the collective government view. G. H. Jones has argued that there is always a danger that other ministers will 'go native' and see government through blinkered departmental eyes. The Prime Minister is therefore 'the guardian of collective government against the danger immanent in British government of rampant departmentalism' (*Contemporary Record* April 1990).

It is unusual to take votes in Cabinet. Most Prime Ministers have sought to gain the general sense of the meeting ('collecting the voices' in Attlee's phrase), summarize the discussion and draw conclusions. This is often more than a simple reflection of the views of others, for the Prime Minister's own opinions will usually be known and carry weight and the summary can be crucial. A piece of vintage Macmillan illustrates this. His Cabinet was divided on whether to build Concorde. After one inconclusive discussion, when it looked as though the proposal might be defeated, Macmillan decided that it should be deferred to a later meeting. When it came up again he

> was in reminiscent mood. He told his colleagues about his great-aunt's Daimler, which had travelled at 'the sensible speed of thirty miles per hour', and was sufficiently spacious to enable one to descend from it without removing one's top hat. Nowadays, alas! people had a mania for dashing around. But that being so Britain ought to 'cater for this modern eccentricity'. He thought they all really agreed. No one seriously dissented. It was all over in a few minutes. (Bruce-Gardyne and Lawson 1976, p. 28)

Wilson's Cabinets appear to have voted more often than others. There were votes, for example, on the cancellation of the TSR2 aircraft and the sale of arms to South Africa, and Richard Crossman wrote of a tied vote which left Wilson unsure what to do. Denis Healey concluded that Wilson 'was curiously reluctant to lay down the law in cabinet by openly overriding opposition from the majority, as every Prime Minister should from time to time' (Healey 1989, p. 331). Other Prime Ministers have taken occasional votes when there has been a clear and strongly felt split, or if it is important to associate the whole Cabinet with a decision. When Thatcher took a vote before sending the naval task force to the Falklands, Norman Tebbit commented that the 'cabinet is not a place for votes, although if a decision is finely balanced the Cabinet Secretary keeps a tally of views for the Prime Minister's summing up, but that morning the Prime Minister asked each colleague directly, "Should the fleet be dispatched — Yes or No?"' (*Contemporary Record* spring 1989, p. 41).

The Prime Minister creates an atmosphere within the Cabinet.

Macmillan cultivated a relaxed, effortless style. 'He was marvellously entertaining,' said Lord Home, 'You did your business but it was great fun at the same time.' The same could not be said of Eden. His nervy agitated character not only threw its shadow across the Cabinet but filtered down to pervade Whitehall and Westminster. Nor were Heath's Cabinets fun. 'In the cabinet', said an insider, 'he would sit there glowering and saying practically nothing. The colleagues would watch him to see what impression their words were making. Then he would come down one way or another and that was it' (Hennessy 1986, pp. 59 and 77). Until near the end of his premiership Callaghan gave his Cabinets purpose and confidence which brought his colleagues together, whereas Thatcher's early Cabinets were often stormy. Prior claimed that she worked by challenge and confrontation and he confessed that it was not to his taste, especially when challenged by a woman. Thatcher confirmed the style in her reply to Prior's resignation in 1984. 'I take your point about frankness,' she wrote, 'That's what cabinets are for, and lively discussions usually lead to good decisions' (Jenkins 1987, p. 183).

The Cabinet's place within the machinery of government is also influenced by the Prime Minister. Attlee's crisp, efficient style meant that decisions were made quickly and clearly based on papers from the departments, but there were few broad policy discussions. In contrast, Churchill's Cabinets were not 'efficient' but they did concern themselves with the grand sweep of policy, and Churchill, who believed strongly 'in the sanctity of Cabinet government', practised collective decision-making using the full Cabinet. He was proud to boast that in the year to April 1953 he had called 110 meetings compared with Attlee's 85 in a similar period (Hennessy and Seldon 1987, p. 74). Heath tried to reconcile the dual demands of day-by-day decisions and policy-making by calling special sessions at Chequers to survey the broader issues.

Thatcher usually only called one Cabinet meeting each week and cut the number of committees and the flow of Cabinet papers. These actions were interpreted in different ways. one view was that she streamlined the system and made it more effficient by concentrating on major items. The other was that she downgraded the Cabinet so that she could exercise her personal authority by dealing with ministers on a bilateral basis. There was an element of truth in both views, but according to Anthony Seldon the change in the frequency and pattern of Cabinet activity had started before Thatcher. The sea change from a regular two Cabinets to one per week came in the early 1970s, as more work was delegated to Cabinet committees because of the increasing weight of government business and the demands of EEC and other international meetings. According to Seldon, when Burke Trend stood down as Cabinet secretary in 1973, the full Cabinet was still the critical decision-making body, but by the time John Hunt, his successor, retired in 1979, shortly after Thatcher came to power, the principal committees were taking many of the main decisions.

Seldon concluded that Thatcher's Cabinets were less decision-making bodies than coordinators of business and reconcilers of conflict. He found that business was divided between standing items for which no papers were circulated and *ad hoc* subjects which had papers in advance, cleared, if necessary, by the Treasury. The standing items, based on reports from the respective ministers, were the parliamentary business for the coming week, home affairs, foreign affairs and EEC business. Typically there would be between one and four *ad hoc* items covering such matters as key economic questions, crises or matters not resolved in committee (*Public Administration* spring 1990).

Although Prime Ministers have been the leading figures in their Cabinets they have not always gained their way. Their powers have varied according to personality and circumstances. A relatively modest man like Home, who in any case inherited an experienced Cabinet, had much less ambition to impose his will than an obdurate figure like Heath. However, even strong characters have found the Cabinet, or some of its senior members, opposed to them. Lord Alexander noted how Churchill would use charm and pull rank to gain his way and if such tactics failed he would delay a decision in the hope of later success. But at times the Cabinet overruled him, as in January 1952 over the timing of a speech to the nation and in December

1953 over the release of £5m to Egypt, but most notably in a fierce clash in July 1954 when ministers insisted that the Prime Minister should have cleared with them a proposal to meet Soviet leaders. It was, said one member, 'an important act of policy on which the cabinet should have been consulted', and eventually the Prime Minister was forced to apologize (Gilbert 1988, p. 1024). Especially in her early days, Thatcher also faced opposition and defeats. For example, in 1980 Lord Carrington, the Foreign Secretary, insisted that an agreement with the EEC, which Thatcher opposed, should be brought to the Cabinet and there it was endorsed. In those early days she also had to give way to the Cabinet on pay rises for MPs, the scale of public spending cuts in 1981, gas prices and (while Prior was at Employment) on union legislation. Later she had a tighter grip on her colleagues.

Finally, although Prime Ministers have influenced the part that Cabinet plays in government they have not altered the institutional structure. The balance has fluctuated between the assertiveness of individual Prime Ministers and the Cabinet's collegiality, but 'Cabinet government' remains in place even if its precise role has varied.

Committees and Inner Cabinets

There is a network of Cabinet committees which is so active and has become so important that the Cabinet is now often best understood as a system of committees coordinated by the full Cabinet. There are various types of committee. Some are permanent; others are *ad hoc* (called to handle a particular issue); some consist only of ministers; others are a mixture of ministers and civil servants. The Prime Minister is responsible for establishing the committees, deciding on their membership and who chairs them, but the committee system is so firmly entrenched that no Prime Minister would consider trying to work without it, and the choice of members is often dictated by the ministers' posts rather than the personal decision of the Prime Minister. The main standing committees, such as Economic

Affairs and Overseas and Defence, are so busy that much of their business is channelled into their own sub-committees.

Although the committee system is firmly entrenched, Prime Ministers are in a strong position. As well as deciding membership they have the opportunity to create new committees. For example, in October 1968, in addition to the main standing committees, Crossman identified important committees chaired by Wilson, from which he (Crossman) was excluded. These dealt with the constitution and Rhodesia. Crossman accused Wilson of using such groups to circumvent the full Cabinet, and on Rhodesia he claimed that it 'is dealt with by the PM and his closest friends and then presented as a "fait accompli" to cabinet' (Crossman 1977, p. 243). Yet Crossman was unfair to Wilson if he was suggesting that this was unusual for previous and subsequent Prime Ministers have used the same device. Wilson, did, however, enhance the work of the committees by introducing a procedure whereby committee decisions were assumed to have been accepted by the full Cabinet unless directly challenged.

In 1985 Peter Hennessy identified at least 160 committees. At that time the Prime Minister informed the House that she chaired two of the main standing committees – Overseas and Defence Policy, and Economic Strategy – while Lord Whitelaw chaired Home and Social Affairs and John Biffen (Leader of the House) the Legislation committee. According to Hennessy, however, Thatcher also chaired the Intelligence committee, and a number of *ad hoc* groups concerned with the Falklands and Hong Kong, the purchase of an anti-radar missile, the abolition of the GLC and metropolitan counties, the miners' strike, the future of the welfare state, inner cities and the teachers' dispute (Hennessy 1986, pp. 26–31).

On a less formal basis some but not all premiers have created 'inner Cabinets'. These are small informal bodies of ministers, and are distinct from 'kitchen Cabinets' which is the name given to groups of friends and confidants who cluster round a Prime Minister. Inner Cabinets have been established in times of crisis. Both Eden and Thatcher set up small war Cabinets to deal with Suez and the Falklands, but while Eden did not always inform the full Cabinet, Thatcher was 'punctilious about keeping full cabinet informed about major developments and consulted them before implementing the bigger decisions' (Hennessy 1986, p. 119). At other times Prime Ministers have used inner Cabinets more flexibly for general purposes — as sounding boards to discuss policy and form views outside the formal machinery of government. Because an inner Cabinet is not fixed it may be active at some times but inactive at others. The membership is also flexible, based on seniority and/or those whom the Prime Minister values and trusts. Attlee relied on Bevin, Morrison, Dalton and Cripps, who, together with himself, were known as the Big Five. There have been accusations that inner Cabinets are designed to enhance the premier's personal position. Wilson was accused of this when, after policy clashes, he dropped Tony Crosland in 1968 and James Callaghan in 1969 from his inner Cabinet, but usually they are more a way of informal consultation than a personal prop for the premier.

8 Civil Servants and Advisers

In addition to their work in Cabinet some Prime Ministers have sought improvements in the machinery of government and greater efficiency in the civil service. However, the picture has been mixed. Some have shown little interest whereas others have been active, including Heath. He set out to produce a streamlined, efficient administration by reducing the number of departments from 17 to 15 (creating in the process two giant departments: Environment, and Trade and Industry), reducing the size of the Cabinet from 21 to 18, and cutting the number of ministers outside the Cabinet from 33 to 23. At the same time he introduced into government a programme analysis and review scheme of 'management by objectives', he transferred some functions from departments to government agencies, and he created the 'Think Tank' (the Central Policy Review Staff) to review government strategy and policies.

As far as the civil service is concerned, despite intermittent enthusiasm for improvement, and despite criticism from the 'left' that it is class-based and from the 'right' that it is self-seeking, Prime Ministers have usually accepted the civil service's self-perception as a loyal vehicle giving objective advice to its political masters and implementing their decisions irrespective of political colour. Such confidence was reaffirmed as early as 1945 when Attlee took to Potsdam the same officials who days before had served Churchill, and that tradition continued. However Cabinet colleagues and political advisers have not always shown such confidence in the civil service. That was especially noticeable during the Wilson government of 1964–70, when among others Marcia Williams (Wilson's Political Secretary) and Tony Benn accused the 'conservative' civil service of failing to support the ministers, and later they explained government's failures in terms of civil service obstructiveness.

Although in their direct working relations with civil servants Prime Ministers have normally had regular contact only with a few top mandarins and the staff at No. 10, potentially they have a powerful role affecting the whole service. This comes both from their influence on the machinery of government and their powers of patronage. In exercising their patronage premiers have usually followed the 'established channels' for civil service promotions. However, there was controversy during Mrs Thatcher's premiership. She took a close interest in appointments and was accused by critics of promoting civil servants who share her political views. This was unfair, for she relied heavily on the advice of the head of the civil service, and if she revealed preference it was determined more by the style and personality of the officials than their political conviction, for she prefered those who adopted a 'problem-solving' rather than a 'range of options' approach, the 'doers', not the 'contemplators'. Further, if she had wanted to emphasize political conviction she would have been forced to move outside the normal civil service channels, which, as table 8.1 reveals, she did not. Kevin Theakston concluded: 'Mrs Thatcher's Permanent Secretaries seem in background and career experience to be identikit mandarins of the type who have long found their way to the top of the civil service' (*Contemporary Record* April 1990).

Yet, although Thatcher can be absolved from the accusation of consciously politicizing the civil service, Lord Bancroft, who was Head of the Civil Service until 1981, spoke later of the dangers of service to a conviction government giving the 'impression' of a politicized service, and that young officials might discover that advice which ministers wanted to hear was received with so much more enthusiasm than unwelcome advice that they would tend to trim, to 'make their advice what ministers want to hear rather than what they need to know' (*Contemporary Record* summer 1988, p. 3).

Table 8.1 Permanent secretaries and their experience

	Callaghan (*January 1979*)		*Thatcher* (*January 1990*)	
Total number of permanent secretaries	23		20	
Average age on appointment	52.7 years		52.4 years	
Average prior Whitehall service	27.6 years		28.3 years	
	No.	*%*	*No.*	*%*
Oxbridge	17	73.9	15	75.0
Private office experience	17	73.9	19	95.0
Treasury experience	9	39.1	8	40.0
Cabinet office (including CPRS) experience	11	47.8	9	45.0
Stint in No. 10	2	8.7	5	25.0

Apart from the debate about politicization there were two ways in which Thatcher consciously set out to change the civil service. First, she was determined to reduce its size. As table 8.1 reveals the number of permanent secretaries was reduced between 1979 and 1990 from 23 to 20, and that reduction was reflected at all levels. Between 1979 and 1987 the civil service was cut from 732,000 to 600,000. Second, she was determined to improve efficiency. To achieve that she appointed Lord Rayner of Marks and Spencer, and gave him her full backing. He was, she said, 'a remarkable and wonderful person'. Rayner's reforms included a reduction of paperwork (27,000 forms were scrapped and 41,000 redesigned), an improvement in individual performances, and, most difficult of all, a reorientation of the civil service culture to reflect more the 'profit and loss' discipline of the private sector. Rayner's financial management initiative went some way along that road, but in the eyes of Sir Robin Ibbs from ICI, who replaced Rayner, it was still short of the fundamental change required and so Ibbs put forward more radical proposals – 'The Next Steps'. These recommended that the civil service be divided into a small 20,000 policy-making core, while the remaining 580,000, who are responsible for delivering goods and services, should be seen as a series of businesses and therefore split into separate agencies inside or outside the public service. Although Mrs Thatcher responded rather cautiously to the 'Next Step' proposals, experiments in establishing agencies began, so that Peter Hennessy could conclude that: 'Whatever the fate of "The Next Steps", Mrs Thatcher has already had more impact on the management of the civil service than "any" previous prime minister,' without he argued, altering its commitment to serve loyally whatever government is in power (*Contemporary Record* summer 1988, p. 4).

Civil Service Advisers and the Cabinet Office

There is no Prime Minister's Department and in its absence the main sources of civil service support come from the Cabinet Office, the civil servants based at No. 10, and the Civil Service Department (when it has existed). In addition Prime Ministers have regular contact with the senior officials in the Treasury and the Foreign Office and the heads of the intelligence serviecs (MI5 and MI6).

Relations between Prime Ministers and the civil servants who work directly with them have usually been cordial and in some cases very close. Heath perhaps more than any gave the impression of enjoying the company of officials and feeling more at home with them than with his political colleagues, and it was he who introduced mixed Cabinet committees of ministers and officials. Heath put great trust in Sir William Armstrong, the head of the civil service, who, among other things, was charged with responsibility for prices and incomes policy and industrial relations. Dubbed 'Deputy Prime Minister' by the union leaders, Armstrong accompanied Heath to most of the key negotiating sessions. For example, he was with Heath at a meeting with the President of the National Union of Miners which Heath had kept secret from the Cabinet.

Sir William Armstrong was head of the Civil Service Department, but that department, formed in 1968, was abolished in 1981 and the management of the civil service was once again shared between the Treasury and the Cabinet Office. The Cabinet Office, which is usually the chief source of formal advice for the Prime Minister, is at the heart of the government. Its tasks include servicing the Cabinet (preparing agendas, recording minutes, arranging meetings); providing facilities for the whole administration (e.g. the Central Statistical Office); coordinating government activities (such as chairing inter-departmental meetings); and advising the Prime Minister. In the view of Anthony Seldon, who studied the work of the Cabinet Office under Thatcher between 1979 and 1987, its 'political' influence is often exaggerated, for the main aim of the officials is to ensure that the Cabinet's processes and machinery work effectively and efficiently. Crossman and Benn often complained that Wilson 'fixed' the minutes with the Cabinet Office to ensure that the Prime Minister's view prevailed. Wilson denied that, and Anthony Seldon found that while officials gave briefs to the Prime Minister – covering the items that were to be discussed, how the meeting might be handled and the possible outcomes they also prepared the minutes for circulation without their being cleared by the Prime Minister.

The Cabinet Office is led by the Cabinet secretary, who has often formally been designated 'head of the civil service'. For example, when the Civil Service Department was abolished in 1981, the Cabinet secretary became head of the civil service and took responsibility for recommending senior appointments to the Prime Minister. However, the Cabinet secretary has an ambiguous position. He is the servant of the Cabinet as a collective body but also the Prime Minister as its chairman and head of government (so that he has sometimes been seen as the premier's permanent secretary). Sir Robert Armstrong (as distinct from Sir William) was so close to Thatcher that she referred to him as 'My oracle', whereas Lord Trend, after retiring as Cabinet secretary, declared: 'He's not the Prime Minister's exclusive servant. He's the servant of the full cabinet' (Hennessy 1986, p. 20). The diversity and potential ambiguity of the post was explained in 1989 by Sir Robert's successor,

Sir Robin Butler. 'It is certainly', he said,

> the permanent secretary who is nearest to the Prime Minister, and on civil service matters, where the Prime Minister is the Minister for the Civil Service, as head of the Civil Service, I suppose I am her permanent secretary. But on the Cabinet Secretary side of the job, my relationship to the Prime Minister is that of the secretary to the chairman and I serve her in the setting of the agenda and in briefing her for cabinet discussions. As secretary I also serve the cabinet as a whole. (*Contemporary Record* April 1990).

Despite the potential ambiguity and the diversity of personalities, relations between Premiers and Cabinet secretaries have usually been good. Since 1945 three secretaries have each served four Prime Ministers: Sir Norman Brook held the post under Attlee, Churchill, Eden and Macmillan, and was followed by Sir Burke Trend who in his ten years served Macmillan, Home, Wilson and Heath. Next came Sir John Hunt who worked under Heath, Wilson, Callaghan and Thatcher. The only Cabinet secretary to have completed his service under one Prime Minister was Sir Robert Armstrong, who worked for Thatcher from 1979 to 1987, since when Sir Robin Butler has held the post under Thatcher and Major.

Peter Hennessy has divided Cabinet secretaries into 'efficient machine minders' and 'more artistic policy-makers', depending on the personalities and individual strengths of the premier and the secretary, but there is much overlap. For example, Norman Brook, a 'machine minder', paid great attention to procedures, but he also provided 'steering briefs' for the Prime Minister which suggested the order of business at meetings, the points that needed to be brought out in discussion and the outcome that would be most desirable. It is open to question whether Brook was reading the mind of the Prime Minister and the Cabinet or whether he was trying to shape policy. Burke Trend who followed was a 'policy-maker', a man of great courtesy and warmth, immensely cool under pressure, who was reputed to draft white papers in his head. His view, as noted above, was that the secretary should serve the whole Cabinet and yet he disliked the Prime Minister having alternative sources of advice, because for him the Cabinet Office was the 'centre round which the rest of the official machine can come together' (Hennessy 1986, pp. 17–29).

Of Thatcher's Cabinet secretaries, Seldon concluded that while Hunt, a man of great energy and drive, was her tutor in her early months, Armstrong was a faithful servant. His influence was limited because of the Prime Minister's strong convictions and her experience, nevertheless his daily contacts, his briefings and his knowledge of the machinery of government gave him considerable potential for influence and he not only accompanied the Prime Minister to many meetings, including summits, but he was given personal responsibilities, such as leading the negotiating team for the Anglo-Irish Accord in 1985, and other tasks he would wish to have avoided, such as the court hearings in Australia about the *Spycatcher* book (*Public Administration* spring 1990).

In addition to the Cabinet Office, further formal support for the Prime Minister and Cabinet was proved for a time by the Central Policy Review Staff (CPRS or 'Think Tank'). Formed by Heath in 1971 and composed half of civil servants and half of 'outsiders', its tasks were to undertake research into long-term issues and to examine broad policy. However, again there was ambiguity. Was the CPRS to undertake background research with a low profile or was it to advance high-profile initiatives? Was it to serve the whole government or the premier? Favoured by Heath, and led by the powerful and independent Lord Rothschild, it had a high profile, undertook regular investigations and every six months made a general presentation to the Cabinet. Yet, although it set out to be of service to the whole government, its position depended on the Prime Minister, and while Heath's immediate successors retained the CPRS it became less prominent and narrower in its interests until eventually Thatcher wound it up in 1983.

Inside No. 10

Inside No. 10 the Prime Minister has further civil service backing in the form of the Private Office, which is located immediately next to the Cabinet room where Prime Ministers usually work. It is composed of five or six high-flying civil servants who are seconded from their departments as private secretaries to the Prime Minister, and is led by a principal private secretary who coordinates and oversees the work of the office. There is always one secretary from the Foreign Office and at least one from the Treasury. The secretaries arrange the Prime Minister's government activities; act as 'gatekeepers' by deciding who and what reaches the premier; prepare parliamentary business; and they often become a source of day-by-day advice. In carrying out their tasks they have to ease and facilitate the flow of business but they are more than mere cyphers and organizers. 'If they are nothing outside Whitehall', wrote a Foreign Office official, 'the top private Secretaries at No. 10 are very important figures within that hidden yet imposing world. They have no political responsibilities. They are not even accountable to any government department. But they have the ear and eye of the Prime Minister and that is enough to give them immense influence' (Henderson 1984, p. 114). Most private secretaries stay for two or three years but some become entrenched and are especially influential.

The experience of the private secretaries from the Foreign Office is instructive for their role has varied substantially. Bernard Donoughue, writing of his time in No. 10 with Wilson and Callaghan, drew a clear distinction between FCO officials and others. He said that the three FCO men who served in his time 'all seemed a little set apart from the rest of us in No. 10 . . . . Somehow they never ceased to be Foreign Office representatives to the Prime Minister. The other private Secretaries were unreservedly the Prime Minister's men' (Donoughue 1987, p. 19). Yet some FCO officials have clearly become 'the Prime Minister's men'. One of these, Philip Zulueta, stayed in No. 10 for no less than nine years, serving Eden, Macmillan and Home and sacrificing his chances in the Foreign Office. Another long server, Charles Powell, worked so closely with Thatcher and become so influential that he was an object of press and parliamentary attention, and even bitterness among some Foreign Office colleagues. He too was described as 'Deputy Prime

Minister', and even 'the son that Mrs Thatcher never had'.

Another important office in No. 10 is that of the press secretary. The holders of this office have fallen into a border area between officials and non-officials. Of the 16 who served between 1945 and 1990, some had previously been civil servants, others journalists and some had been both. For example, Francis Williams, who worked for Attlee, had experience of both, whereas Joe Haines was a journalist brought in by Wilson with no civil service experience; Callaghan and Heath used civil servants – Tom McCaffrey and Donald Maitland respectively. The press secretary's main tasks are to act as spokesman for the Prime Minister and the government; to advise on media relations (including the premier's speeches); to act as intermediary between the government and the media; and finally to coordinate the information services. He is therefore pulled in many directions; 'between the Prime Minister and the other members of the cabinet; the politicians and the civil service; between the Prime Minister and cabinet and the Press' (C. Seymour-Ure, *Contemporary Record* autumn 1989). In attempting to reconcile this, some Prime Ministers have separated out the political side of the task by appointing a minister responsible for information or a separate party press officer as Wilson did with Gerald Kaufman.

Handling the media not infrequently leads to controversy, and that reached a peak with Bernard Ingham who served Thatcher. Before coming to No. 10 Ingham had had both journalistic and civil service experience, including a spell as Tony Benn's information officer when Benn was in the Labour Cabinet. A number of reasons explain the controversy surrounding Ingham. First, he served longer than any other press secretary (only Harold Evans' seven years with Macmillan comes near to Ingham's 11 with Thatcher). Second, increased television coverage gave him a personal prominence. Third, most of the time he had to cover the full range of the job because there was no political appointment. Finally, he used his aggressive, bullying style to forward Thatcher's interests. He was accused, for instance, of using the lobby system to do Thatcher's dirty work by undermining Cabinet colleagues who had earned her displeasure.

John Biffen was dismissed shortly after Ingham described him as a 'semi-detached member of the Cabinet', and Francis Pym also disappeared from the scene soon after Thatcher had defended him in parliament while Ingham was describing him as 'Mona Lott' in an off-the-record briefing. In contrast those whom Thatcher favoured, like Major, were given kind words.

Policy units also fall along the 'official/non-official' boundary, That was the case with the small policy unit which Wilson set up in 1974 to be his 'eyes and ears'. The leader, Bernard Donoughue, an academic and Labour supporter, was given a civil service post. He explained that the unit was to look at short- and medium-term issues and had three main characteristics: 'It was systematic, it was separate from the Whitehall machine, and it was working solely for the Prime Minister' (Donoughue 1987, p. 20). The unit was retained by Callaghan, and with changed personnel by Thatcher.

Family, Friends and Advisers

In the scramble for the Prime Minister's attention, Cabinet members, ministers and civil servants are joined by political appointees, experts and personal friends. In their day-to-day activities Prime Ministers are flanked on one side by the world of government and administration through the civil service; and on the other the world of politics through political advisers. In some cases the political advisers have been introduced as a counter-balance to the civil servants' power.

While there is continuity among many of the civil servants, Prime Ministers also draw around them people they trust personally, because of their judgement and expertise and/or because they feel at ease with them and value them as individuals. Thus a change in the premiership means a change of personnel. For example, as soon as Major moved into No. 10 he replaced Bernard Ingham with Gus O'Donnell, who had been his press secretary at the Treasury, and he replaced Professor Brian Griffiths as head of the policy unit with Sarah Hogg, an economic journalist.

Sometimes these advisers have acted as individuals and sometimes as a loose group or 'kitchen Cabinet'. The advisers have had diverse backgrounds: party members, academics, media people, family and friends. Thatcher turned to experts both from inside the civil service, like Anthony Parsons from the Foreign Office, and non-officials like Alan Walters, a professor of economics. Other Prime Ministers have brought in party supporters, as Heath did with Douglas Hurd. For some, family and friends have provided the support they need. Churchill was exceptionally well supported, when, following a stroke in 1953, his family and personal followers rallied to his help. His son-in-law Christopher Soames and his private secretaries, Jock Colville and David Pitblado — with the connivance of the family, senior ministers, senior civil servants and media barons — not only kept secret the Prime Minister's condition but covered much of his work. Churchill also like to relax with a set of personal friends, his 'cronies', such as Lord Moran (his doctor), Lord Cherwell and Brendan Bracken. Macmillan brought into the Private Office John Wyndham, a trusted friend who served in an unofficial and unpaid capacity, and Wilson turned to a 'kitchen Cabinet' which included Marcia Williams, party associates such as George Wigg and Gerald Kaufman and 'experts' like Tommy Balogh and Nick Kaldor. Whatever the Prime Minister's choice these advisers help to ease the loneliness of the government's most senior position.

With so much competition to gain attention and exert influence, Prime Ministers often received conflicting advice. For instance, in 1978 the policy unit and the Treasury gave Callaghan different views on an acceptable prices and incomes policy. Such differences are natural and when a collegiate spirit develops are accepted without acrimony among the groups and individuals around the premier. However, bitterness can arise, as in Wilson's 'kitchen Cabinet'. In that case much of the controversy concerned the Prime Minister's political adviser Marcia Williams (later Lady Falkender) who exercised great influence on Wilson. Joe Haines, the Press Secretary, was among her strongest critics. He claimed that her influence was 'all pervasive . . . . No one who worked in his (Wilson's) office for more than a few minutes could be unaware of it. Every typist and every civil servant knew of it and could testify to it. Many of them went in dread of her; the fact of her power was like a baleful cloud hung permanently over their heads' (Haines 1977, p. 157). According to Haines, Wilson relied on Williams and gave her concerns first priority, which adversely affected the conduct of government and was one of the burdens that wore him out. Not surprisingly Williams and Wilson rejected these accusations and criticized Haines.

The battles among Wilson's advisers were conducted in the shadows. A more open clash came in Thatcher's government which led to the resignation of Nigel Lawson, the Chancellor of the Exchequer. The immediate issue at stake was a difference over British entry into the European Exchange Rate System, but, after his resignation in 1989 Lawson claimed that this was 'the tip of a singularly ill-concealed iceberg'. The bulk of the iceberg, he said, consisted of a decision-making process whereby the views of an adviser, Alan Walters, were publicly known to be at variance with those of himself as Chancellor. Lawson said that he had objected on many occasions to Walters' conduct, and before resigning 'I explained to her (Thatcher) that so long as Alan Walters remained as her personal economic adviser, conducting himself in the way he did and holding the views that he was known to hold, then my position as Chancellor was untenable' (*Independent* 6 November 1989). Thatcher's response to Lawson and to those who questioned her behaviour was that advisers are there to give free and honest views, but ministers take the decisions and they did so in her government. However, when she took no steps to remove Walters the Chancellor resigned, reawakening the debate about the way in which Thatcher conducted government business. Consciously or unconsciously she had underlined the point that whenever a Prime Minister seeks advice, whatever its source and content, it is he/she who decides whether or not to accept it. The buck stops with the Prime Minister and not the adviser, whether he be Chancellor of the Exchequer or a professor of economics.

Executive Groups

In drawing together the discussion of the Cabinet, civil servants and advisers, it is helpful to turn to Patrick Dunleavy and R. A. W. E. Rhodes who have argued that the concept of 'Cabinet government' should be replaced with that of a 'core executive'. They argue that the picture of the Cabinet working as a single unit and controlling all the government's activities is based on an unrealizable ideal (what 'should' happen) and not on actual practice. The 'core executive' proposed by Dunleavy and Rhodes comprises not only the Prime Minister, the Cabinet and its committees, but the departments of government and senior civil servants (*Public Administration* spring 1990).

A modified version of the 'core executive' can be applied here to explain the Prime Minister's relations with the Cabinet and advisers. The formal structure of the Cabinet and its committees can play an important part in the executive, and sometimes the conventional picture operates with the Cabinet acting as a unit directing government activity, especially when there is serious dispute in the government. However, usually a better understanding of the executive and the Prime Minister's role in it can be gained, first, by moving beyond the formal picture of Cabinet government, and, second, by downgrading dividing lines between the Cabinet, departments, officials and other advisers. Premiers form and use 'executive groups' which interact with the Cabinet and its committees. The composition and task of the groups vary with circumstances and the wishes and needs of each Prime Minister. In terms of circumstances, obvious examples are the economic seminar which Callaghan formed to respond to the economic problems of the day and Thatcher's war Cabinet during the Falklands campaign. In terms of composition the groups will depend on the expertise that is required and the premier's personal preferences – as well as ministers Callaghan brought in economics experts to help his seminar; Thatcher turned to the service chiefs to advise on the Falklands; Wilson's teams included members of his 'kitchen Cabinet'; Heath relied on senior civil servants and Thatcher on her officials in No. 10.

The group concept is fluid and flexible. Some groups are offshoots of the Cabinet and its committees, others are more widely drawn. Some are created for specific purposes, like the Falklands, but others have a more general role covering a range of topics, as was the case with the inner Cabinets employed by Attlee, Wilson and Heath. Usually several groups will be operating at the same time, sometimes with overlapping menbership and overlapping concerns. On occasion those who believe they have a legitimate interest are excluded, and that can produce conflict. George Brown complained that he was excluded from groups that were taking decisions within his ministerial responsibility. He therefore appealed to the conventional constitutional view, claiming that Wilson was flouting 'Cabinet government'. There were similar situations during Thatcher's premiership. The Westland helicopter dispute is one example. It boiled down to who should decide whether Westland, which needed bailing out by the government, should cooperate with an American company or a European consortium. Had the decision not created a major conflict between Thatcher and the independently minded Michael Heseltine it would probably have been made by one of the Prime Minister's groups and passed through the Cabinet on the nod. As it was, the dispute created a major row involving the Cabinet, a Cabinet committee, several departments of government, individual ministers, the government's law officers and officials in No. 10. Heseltine's accusations were similar to Brown's, that the Prime Minister had flouted Cabinet government, and because of that she was forced to turn to the full Cabinet for support, but not without sacrificing another Cabinet member, Leon Brittan. When there are such disputes the conventional view of Cabinet government tends to be emphasized, with all sides claiming that they are acting within the convention.

While there are such disputes more often the interplay of groups operates effectively. Indeed a premier's influence within the government is to extent dependent on his/her success in forming and using groups. For example, Martin Burch has pointed out how in the early part of Thatcher's premiership, when she was facing strong opposition on economic matters, she largely succeeded in keeping economic policy outside the full Cabinet and within her chosen groups. In the first 14 months of her administration economic policy-making was conducted in a Cabinet committee (where she had ministers sympathetic to her) and in groups such as the No. 10 policy unit. Apart from discussions on expenditure reviews, the Cabinet as a body did not consider general economic strategy, and so the Prime Minister was able to push ahead with her policy despite the scepticism of many Cabinet members (*Parliamentary Affairs* vol. 36 no. 4).

9 Economic Policy

Prime Ministers are involved in policy-making across the board. Yet within the vast range of government activity there are areas in which they participate only intermittently, if at all. In others they are active in times of difficulty, or from personal interests or party priorities. Some policy areas, however, are of constant and central concern to government. These include economic policy which is discussed in this chapter, and foreign policy which is discussed in the next.

Economic Policy – a Growing Involvement

Since 1945 concern over the economy has been a persistent feature of British politics – dominating elections, leading to clashes between and within parties and between the government and organized labour. Each government came to realize that its ability to achieve its goals rested largely on economic strength or weakness. Prime Ministers, who are formally First Lords of the Treasury, have all played a part in economic policy-making, but their contribution has varied according to their ability, commitment and the circumstances of the time. They entered the scene with different experiences and background. Only Wilson was a trained economist; three (Churchill, Macmillan and Callaghan) had served as Chancellors of the Exchequer; but others, notably Attlee, Eden and Home, had little economic background.

Generally, the premier's role has increased during the period. While in the early years Prime Ministers could often keep themselves at arm's length that was not the case by the time Callaghan became Prime Minister in 1976. Although he resolved not to 'over-involve' himself in economic policy, and to leave it to the Chancellor, 'I found', he wrote, 'as I suppose other Prime Ministers have done, that economic problems obtrude at every street corner, and despite my good intentions there were periods when they occupied large slices of my time' (Callaghan 1987, p. 399). The growing involvement can be traced through each Prime Minister.

Attlee's government reshaped the national economy. In a harsh world of rationing and the ever-present 'dollar gap', it translated the post-war commitments to social and economic planning and full employment into policies which created the welfare state and nationalized industries. Attlee presided over this as chairman of the Cabinet and kept himself informed on economic issues, but according to Douglas Jay, his political secretary, Attlee viewed economics like medicine – as something he admired but did not understand. Economic initiatives mainly came from others, and he largely left the management of the economy to his Chancellors (Dalton and Cripps). In the government's first two years Attlee did not chair the Cabinet's economic committee, but he was drawn directly into economic affairs in 1947 – a year of crisis, with severe fuel shortages, and balance of payments and convertibility problems. In those circumstances Attlee took over the committee dealing with fuel, but still did not give an overall lead in economic management. As the crisis deepened, the Prime Minister often seemed 'impenetrable and impervious' (Morgan 1984, p. 351). As a result, plots were hatched to remove him, but the plots failed and Attlee showed his astuteness by giving more power to one of the plotters (Cripps, the Chancellor) and himself taking the chair at a new economic committee, which met weekly and 'became the most important in the system, the one where all the big economic issues – domestic and overseas – were handled' (Hennessy 1986, pp. 44–5). Yet criticism of Attlee persisted. Cripps complained of a lack of crucial economic decision-making, and of policies 'whittled away or referred to further committees. There was no drive at the centre' (Morgan 1984, p. 348). Economic problems continued and, despite austerity and cuts in public expenditure, the government was forced to devalue the pound in 1949. As Cripps was ill Attlee chaired the group which made the decision, but again he let others take the lead, in that case young, economically minded ministers – Gaitskell, Jay and Wilson.

The situation with Churchill was not dissimilar. Despite his experience as Chancellor in the 1920s, he found post-war economic problems bewildering. 'He was not brought up on such things,' wrote Lord Moran (Gilbert 1988, p. 675). He was not one to dwell on detail, which is sometimes required in economic management, and he was frustrated by the restrictions economic conditions imposed on foreign and defence policies. Perhaps Churchill's greatest contribution was a negative one – that he did not attempt to undo the policies of the previous Labour government. Indeed he told he House: 'What the nation needs is several years of quiet steady administration, if only to allow Socialist legislation to reach its full fruition' (Gilbert 1988, p. 659). However, not all the changes of the new economic consensus were to his taste. When the Conservative 'Industrial Charter' was explained to Churchill he said he did not agree with a word of it, but decided not to throw his considerable personal influence against it.

While Churchill had general views, such as favouring a freer economy and keeping the unions happy, he left the bulk of the work to the young Chancellor, Rab Butler. At first Churchill decided that Butler needed help from older heads and appointed Lord Cherwell as Paymaster General to report directly to the Prime Minister. However, Butler emerged as the major figure. He, and not the Prime Minister, chaired the Cabinet's economic policy committee, and he was increasingly given a loose rein in what proved a period of relative economic success. Butler enjoyed the freedom, but he also regretted the absence of a 'coherent guiding hand from the Prime Minister' (Seldon 1981, p. 168). That came home during an exchange rate crisis in 1952 when Butler made a radical proposal for the partial floating of sterling. At first Churchill was sympathetic, wanting to 'set the Pound free', but after consulting others (including Cherwell and Eden who opposed it) he brought it to the Cabinet, where his contribution was that of uncommitted chairman, not policy-maker, and after a heated discussion Butler's proposal was turned down.

The Prime Minister's relatively low-key role in economic matters was challenged for a time by Eden. He was a poor delegator and both his Chancellors of the Exchequer, Butler and Macmillan, were subjected to regular interference. Eden clashed with Butler over budget plans, and later although Macmillan overcame the Prime Minister's opposition to removing bread subsidies, Eden's views prevailed in opposing cuts in RAF expenditure and increasing taxes (Lamb 1987, pp. 54–8). Eden's advice could be sound. For instance, in August 1955 he minuted to Butler: 'We must put the battle against inflation before anything else. If the cost of living were reduced we would be able to speak to both sides of industry... and the Nation will back us up' (Rhodes James, 1986, p. 416). However, Eden was not consistent. For example, despite his earlier advice, Butler complained that he could not gain the Prime Minister's support for severe measures to counter inflation after the 1955 election (Butler 1973, p. 181). Also, despite his clashes with the Treasury, Eden lacked experience and confidence in economic affairs and left Butler and then Macmillan as chairmen of the economic committee. In October 1955 his inexperience showed through when he made an 'ineffective speech' in a major Commons economic debate, finding that a rowdy House was not his scene, 'nor was the economy his subject' (Rhodes James 1986, p. 422). Then, in the last period of his premiership, Eden became so absorbed in the Suez crisis that he played little part in economic policy.

It was in Macmillan's time that the Prime Minister became more overtly involved in economic policy-making. There were several reasons for this. First, the Suez crisis had cruelly exposed the limitations a weak economy imposed on Britain's international position, and Macmillan, who was Chancellor at the time, had been converted overnight from a 'hawk' to a 'dove' by US pressure on sterling. It became clearer than before that although the British economy was growing more quickly than in the past (in the 'never had it so good' years) it was growing more slowly than those of other major Western states. Macmillan tried to counter this relative international decline by repairing relations with the US and seeking (if failing) to gain EEC membership. Second, Macmillan personally had firm economic ideas, based on the misery of unemployment he had witnessed as Member of Parliament for Stockton in the 1920s and 1930s. Determined to avoid a repetition of that, he was committed to growth, even when that was opposed by the Treasury. Third, increased television coverage of politics focused attention on the Prime Minister, who was held responsible for all government activity, not least economic policy.

By the early 1960s, the economic policies of the Macmillan government were in trouble as full employment pushed up the cost of labour, and public expectations were fuelled by rash party promises that the government could manage the economy to achieve ever-improving standards of living. The government's attempts to control the situation by pay pauses and 'stop–go' policies only provided temporary relief. When Macmillan resigned, Home inherited a burden of economic problems, but he sought to distance himself from them. When asked later if he had chaired the economic policy committee, Home replied with disarming frankness: 'Oh no. No, no I wouldn't. The Chancellor of the Exchequer did that. But I used to talk to him (Reginald Maudling) regularly, of course . . . . I was not familiar with economics. They had never come my way.' Home also relied on his principal private secretary, Derek Mitchell. 'I never understood a word about economics,' explained the Prime Minister later, 'and his strength was economics.' Home's limitations were clear to all, including himself, and he was criticized not only by the opposition and the media but by some in his own party. 'If I had thought I was going to be Prime Minister', he said, 'I would have taken more trouble to understand the various theories' (Hennessy 1986, pp. 64–5). Ironically therefore, Home's economic limitations served only to underline that a Prime Minister could no longer avoid a significant involvement in economic policy-making.

In contrast with Home, Wilson came to power in 1964 determined to play a prominent part in economic policy. After what he described as 'thirteen years of Tory misrule', he was in a strong position. He was an economist, his colleagues lacked experience in government and there was much public sympathy for his new broom approach. He set out a dynamic programme, and introduced a new government framework which included a Department of Economic Affairs (DEA) to share responsibility for economic management with the Treasury, and a Prices and Incomes Board, an archetypal Wilson insitution which 'represented the apogee of the expert and of the belief in the powers of problem-solving social science' (Jenkins 1987, p. 11). Wilson also played a direct part in economic management, for example in the early balance of payments crisis when he ended speculation about devaluation by refusing even to have it discussed. He fostered a view that the government was capable of reshaping the country's economic destiny, in which increased public expenditure would play a prominent part. Yet after the warm public response to his early dynamic approach, Wilson was to learn that the government's capabilities were less than he had suggested and that personal involvement exposed the Prime Minister to criticism when things went wrong. And things did go wrong. The DEA made no impact and was eventually abandoned; the Prices and Incomes Board failed to control either prices or incomes; the 'stop – go' pattern persisted; and Wilson, in the face of opposition led by Callaghan, failed to persuade the Cabinet to support proposals for trade union reform ('In Place of Strife'). Finally, the government was forced into devaluation, and Wilson compounded that humiliation by declaring that the pound in the pocket retained its value.

When Heath came to power in 1970 his personal commitment was as great as Wilson's. He was pledged 'to change the course of history of this nation, nothing less', with an economic programme agreed in opposition at Selsdon Park as the centrepiece (Jenkins 1989, p. 13). This rejected a statutory incomes policy, central planning and support for 'lame duck' industries, and instead favoured a tougher, efficient market-orientated system. James Prior, one of Heath's lieutenants, wrote of the Prime Minister's vision in which he would release a fund of energy and investment, and end 'stop–go' economic policies. Alas for Heath: after struggling for two years he succumbed before the pressure of events. He was unlucky in that he had to face the international oil crisis, combined with rising unemployment and militant unions, but whether from circumstance or lack of will Heath's government went into reverse, making a series of dramatic U-turns. By 1972 it was helping 'lame duck' industries, giving itself sweeping new rights of intervention (through the Industry Act), and trying to control pay, prices and dividends. When these failed Heath went to ignominious electoral defeat during a miners' strike which reduced the country to a three-day working week because of lack of fuel.

When Wilson returned to power in 1974 he carried old scars. He knew that economic aims were difficult to achieve, especially for a party committed to retaining full employment and close relations with the unions, and that failure carried a high political cost for the Prime Minister. He inherited an economic crisis (the three-day week and rising inflation), but after a quick settlement of the miners' dispute he left economic problems 'to simmer on back burner'. There was little economic discussion in Cabinet, because Wilson had 'shrewdly learned from long and painful previous experience that if a major economic crisis is looming it is politically better to wait until the seriousness of the situation is unmistakably apparent to one's ministerial colleagues', before asking them to take painful decisions (Donoughue 1987, p. 60). Wilson's initial concern was not about the economy but holding the government together, as it squabbled over EEC membership and devolution. As late as June 1975 he remained neutral when the Chancellor, Healey, proposed substantial public expenditure cuts and, without his backing, the cuts were not made. However, the premier's centrol role in economic matters re-emerged when his authority was needed, first to carry a wages policy through the party and Cabinet, and second to ensure that it was voluntary and not statutory, as the Treasury wanted (King 1985, p. 59).

The experience of Wilson's successor, Callaghan, revealed both the strength and the vulnerability of a Prime Minister in economic policy-making. His central role emerged in the sterling crisis of 1976. The value of the pound fell sharply as doubts increased about the British economy, the steps taken by the Treasury proved ineffective and Britain was forced to turn to the International Monetary Fund (IMF). It was a humiliating situation but Callaghan took the lead. He sought international support from Chancellor Schmidt and President Ford, he advocated (against Treasury advice) removing sterling as a reserve currency and supported a conditional IMF loan. In doing so he performed a balancing act between the IMF, the Treasury and groups within the Cabinet. On one hand he formed 'the seminar', a small body composed of ministers and officials whom he trusted and with whom he discussed sensitive issues, and on the other hand, once he had a position, he was less deferential to the Treasury than Wilson and more open with the Cabinet. Although the crisis threatened to split the government, Callaghan allowed wide-ranging, exhaustive Cabinet debate before he swung the day by throwing his weight behind the Chancellor and a modified IMF package. The Cabinet, faced with a test of loyalty and potentially even greater economic troubles, rallied behind the Prime Minister. Callaghan had succeeded in resisting excessive demands from the IMF, holding the Cabinet together and persuading his colleagues to go far enough to gain the loan. This gave him a powerful position until the winter of 1978/9. That winter − 'the Winter of Discontent' − destroyed Callaghan's government. The Labour administration had claimed a special relationship with the trades unions but when voluntary agreements with the unions collapsed a dispirited and exhausted government floundered in a sea of inflation, strikes and rising unemployment. It finished in 'quiet despair'.

Callaghan's experience following the troubles of Wilson and Heath, raised questions which any future Prime Minister would have to face: had Britain become ungovernable? was the economy so vulnerable to harsh international winds, and/or militant trades unions, and/or poor management, and/or incompetent governments that it could never match other developed countries? When Thatcher won the 1979 election, she had no doubt about the answers to such questions. Her government would transform the economy. Like an Old Testament prophet she said: 'This is my faith. This is what I passionately believe. If you believe it too, then come with me' (Kavanagh and Morris 1989, p. 9). She identified economic policy as a central concern and made clear that although implementation might be left to the Chancellor, she would lay down the ground rules. Thorneycroft, the party chairman, said: 'She knew what she wanted to do before she got into office and there was respect for someone who had a goal and absolute confidence' (Holmes 1985, p. 199). However, initially only a minority in the party and the Cabinet shared he economic views. She countered that first by ensuring the vital ministerial posts were in the 'right' hands; second, by placing reliable civil servants in key positions; third, by using sympathetic advisers (notably John Hoskyns and Alan Walters); fourth, by working with carefully selected committees and *ad hoc* groups; and finally, by personal leadership. She did not always win but she was always prepared to fight.

Although Thatcher's tenacity did not always succeed and her economic aims were only partly fulfilled, there was no doubt about the prominent and direct part she played in economic policy-making. That was underlined by a major confrontation which arose between Thatcher and the Chancellor (Lawson) in the late 1980s over the management of the exchange rate and membership of the European Monetary System (EMS). Backed by Alan Walters, she wanted to leave the pound to the markets ('There is no way you can buck the market,' she claimed) while Lawson favoured management of the pound by intervention and the use of interest rates, and he was sympathetic to the EMS. Lawson had held these views since the mid-1980s but had been unable to persuade the Prime Minister to support him. For a time the conflict was kept out of the Cabinet by Thatcher's characteristic way of dealing with ministers on a bilateral basis, but the dispute became public during 1989, shortly before the budget. Thatcher and Lawson gave contradictory views to the Commons, and the situation was inflamed when Howe (the Foreign Secretary) also came out in favour of the EMS. For a time the row was patched up as Thatcher did a partial climb-down, by giving public support to the Chancellor for limited management of the exchange rate, but she did not abandon her position and the differences re-emerged dramatically later in the year when Lawson resigned after an open dispute.

Prime Minister, Chancellors and the Treasury

As the clash between Thatcher and Lawson revealed, the relationship between the Prime Minister and the Chancellor is central to economic policy-making. The Prime Minister starts with the advantage of choosing the Chancellor. Some have chosen strong figures, as Wilson did with Jenkins and Healey; others, like Macmillan, have chosen compliant figures; and others, as with Thatcher, those who largely (if not entirely) shared their views. Whatever the choice, the relationship is close, and if the Prime Minister and Chancellor are agreed, even controversial issues, like the IMF loan, can be carried. Denis Healey, who was Chancellor for five years, wrote of the loneliness of the job and the problems of telling colleagues that their hopes could not be met. 'Without the support of the Prime Minister (the job) is impossible' (Healey 1989, p. 388). Healey usually received support from Wilson and Callaghan, but there was potential for tension, from different concerns and conflicting agendas. The Chancellor has to 'balance the books', whereas the Prime Minister has to take an overview of the government, seek to hold the party together and win elections, and to achieve these ends may favour a different approach. Healey describes how he proposed to Callaghan in 1976 that interest rates would have to be increased by 2 per cent. When Callaghan opposed this, Healey said he would take it up in the Cabinet, knowing that without the premier's support he would be defeated and have to resign. In the event, Callaghan, conscious of the crisis that would follow, supported Healey.

When such tensions had arisen in Macmillan's time they were not so easily reconciled because there was a conflict of economic views. Influenced, like many of his contemporaries, by the ideas of Maynard Keynes, which had been reinforced by his Stockton experience, Macmillan was an expansionist. This brought clashes with his Chancellors, who, backed by the Treasury sought to counter inflation by holding down public expenditure. The first clash in 1958 was spectacular. All three Treasury ministers resigned, led by Thorneycroft, the Chancellor. Nigel Birch, one of the other Treasury ministers wrote: 'It was a principle of will. You'll never conquer inflation unless you damn well mean to — and Harold hadn't the will' (Horne 1989, p. 76). Privately Macmillan was concerned but publicly he dismissed the affair as 'these little local difficulties'. Certainly it did not change his views. He replaced Thorneycroft with the more pliable Heathcoat Amory, who, despite increasing doubts, followed Macmillan's lead. However, the relationship deteriorated and by 1960 Macmillan came away from the pre-budget discussions concerned at Amory's loss of nerve. In the event the Prime Minister's opposition to deflation succeeded in gaining a 'stand-still' budget, against Treasury advice. Soon afterwards Amory resigned, to be replaced by another compliant figure, the faithful Selwyn Lloyd. Lloyd did not directly challenge Macmillan, but, caught between 'Stocktonian Keynesians on the one hand and Treasury orthodoxy on the other', he too showed increasing concern about public expenditure (Thorpe 1989, p. 316). That, and what Macmillan thought was Lloyd's absence of initiative, led to the Chancellor's dismissal in July 1962. Even the criticism directed at Macmillan after that did not deflect him from his economic path. He sent a memo to Maudling, the new Chancellor, calling for a radical attack on economic weaknesses, including the North/South divide, and urging him to introduce a 1963 budget aiming at 'expansion without inflation'.

As Macmillan's experience had shown, the Treasury, an elite department of government, is both admired and feared by Prime Ministers: admired because of the quality of its staff and its corporate spirit; feared because of its influence across the government and its ability to counter political initiatives. Some Prime Ministers have attempted to curb its power by establishing alternative structures for policy-making, including: Attlee's economic committee, which was created so that 'the Treasury was no longer the sole voice on economic policy' (Harris 1982, p. 402); Churchill's Treasury advisory committee of senior ministers and his frustrated attempt to appoint an 'economic overlord'; Wilson's Department of Economic Affairs; and Callaghan's 'seminar'. In forming the DEA Wilson said: 'Britain could hope to win economic security only by a fundamental reconstruction and modernization of industry under the direction of a department as least as powerful as the Treasury' (Wilson 1974, p. 24). Yet none of these efforts succeeded in undermining the Treasury's powerful position in the machinery of government.

In Wilson's time there were constant complaints from other departments and his own 'kitchen Cabinet' about the Treasury's power. Crossman spoke of its 'domination', based on representatives strategically placed in every department who find it difficult 'not to feel a greater loyalty to the Treasury than to their Minister' (Crossman 1976, p. 200). Joe Haines, the press secretary, accused the Treasury of claiming infallibility, of being anti-Labour and of never accepting defeat because ministers come and go but the Treasury goes on for ever. However Wilson, although accused by his own advisers of being in awe of the Treasury and being too ready to accept its view, not only set up the DEA (albeit unsuccessfully), but sought alternative economic advice from a minister (Harold Lever) and from the No. 10 policy unit. Sometimes Wilson acted against Treasury advice, as towards the end of his premiership when there was a dispute over wages in which the Treasury supported a statutory policy while the policy unit backed a voluntary approach. After vacillating, Wilson came down in favour of the voluntary policy which was then approved by the Cabinet.

The conclusion must be that when the Prime Minister is working in harmony with the Chancellor and the Treasury they form a virtually irresistible force. However, when there are differences each has a capacity to frustrate the others. While the Treasury does play a central role in government these are cases when Prime Ministers have countered its powers — over control of public expenditure under Macmillan, over devaluation under Wilson and over membership of the European Monetary System under Thatcher.

Consensus and Conviction

Between 1945 and 1979 there was a loose political consensus: 'a set of parameters which bounded the set of policy options regarded by senior politicians and civil servants as administratively practicable, economically affordable and politically acceptable' (Kavanagh and Morris 1989, p. 13). The consensus was both of substance and style. The substance was created by the Attlee government, based on a mixed economy, major nationalized industries, full employment and welfare provision. The style was a search for broad agreement by conciliating major interests, by compromise and by gaining the political 'middle ground'. Within the parameters there was disagreement both between parties and within governments, and during the 1970s the consensus was increasingly challenged, but in broad terms it held.

In economic policy the consensus was labelled 'Butskeralism', after two Chancellors (Butler for the Tories and Gaitskell for Labour). The broad vision was a 'social democratic' Britain with a mixed economy, state management for social ends, the pursuit of full employment and a welfare state, but in managing the economy it was always difficult to find the right level between inflation and deflation. 'It was not', said Macmillan, 'a subject to be solved by mathematical formulae, or exact calculation. It was like bicycling along a tightrope' (Horne 1989, p. 65). The efforts of individual Prime Ministers to keep the bicycle on the rope depended on an interplay of their experience, beliefs and political circumstances, but by the 1970s there were clear doubts about whether the old consensus was the right rope along which to cycle, as Heath announced the Selsdon programme and Callaghan told the Labour Party, 'You cannot spend your way out of a recession.' Yet they both failed to make a clear break, because although they had lost faith in the substance of the consensus they were still wedded to the style – the search for compromise and the reconciliation of interests, including the unions.

The walls of the consensus collapsed before Thatcher's convictions. She rejected both its substance and style. 'For me,' she said, 'consensus seems to be the process of abandoning all beliefs and principles, values and policies' (Kavanagh and Morris 1989, p. 2). In its place emerged 'Thatcherism'. This stood for many things: a leadership style; a strong government prepared to resist powerful interests; a reaction against high inflation and trades unions militancy; an ambition to reduce public expenditure; and an emphasis on law and order. Some, like John Vincent, claimed that 'she made up Thatcherism as she went along,' and, for example, privatization was not part of her original programme (Hennessy and Seldon 1987, p. 278). But certainly management of the economy was a major testing ground for the views of a premier whose background was self-reliance, hard work and thrift, whose bad experiences were the strikes and 'stop–goes' of the 1960s and 1970s and whose ideas were influenced by the 'monetarist'.

Thatcher's supporters believed that the search for consensus had created a socialist ratchet effect, whereby each compromise shifted the 'middle ground' to the left. They sought to reverse that by moving from a 'collectivist' society to the 'personal' society. 'Economics', said Thatcher, 'are the method, the object is to change the heart and mind' (Holmes 1985, p. 209). The method involved a reduction of money supply to squeeze out inflation; a reduction in public expenditure; and a free labour market. The objective was to promote individualism, entrepreneurial drive and a free market by removing controls on wages, prices and profits. As a result trades unions were no longer consulted and their powers restricted, the boundaries of the mixed economy were redrawn through privatization, the commitment to full employment was abandoned and 'the nanny state' rejected. Nigel Lawson declared that the chosen course represented 'a distinct and self-conscious break from the predominantly social democratic assumptions that have hitherto underlain policy in post-war Britain' (Kavanagh 1987, p. 13).

Yet, with Heath's and Callaghan's recent experiences in mind, there was scepticism that Thatcher could sustain the break with the past or govern outside the consensus. In 1979 Peregrine Worsthorne, a Conservative writer, concluded: 'Whatever happens in the election is not going to make much difference. There will be neither revolution nor counter-revolution' and change will be measured 'in inches not miles' (Kavanagh 1987, p. 207). He was wrong. He had underestimated Thatcher's determination. In the first two years her government's economic policies were in great trouble, with high inflation, appalling unemployment and a substantial drop in output. Opposition came not only from Labour and unions but within the Conservative Party and from the Confederation of British Industries (CBI). Sir Terence Beckett, the CBI director general, criticized high interest rates and described the Conservative Party as a 'narrow alliance' with no business experience or understanding. Yet, Thatcher refused to change course. 'The lady', she said, 'is not for turning,' and in 1981, despite increasing unemployment and falling output, the government introduced a very tough budget.

The path continued to be difficult and costly, inconsistencies arose as pragmatism and ideology jostled against each other and not all objectives were achieved. Within a year inflation was running at 22 per cent, and while it fell sharply afterwards it rose steadily again after 1988; in the early years large subsidies were paid to nationalized industries; the government did not keep out of industrial disputes; it failed to solve the problems of wage settlements in the public sector and high public expenditure; and after a spurt in the mid-1980s Britain's growth rate again fell behind the leading Western states. The highest price for the changes was paid by the unemployed, whose numbers broke all post-was records, reaching three million in January 1982. A new bitterness entered British politics, culminating in the miners' strike of 1984, and part of that bitterness entered and divided the Conservative Party, most noticeably in the early years. Ian Gilmour, a leading 'wet' wrote to Thatcher after his dismissal in 1981: 'Every Prime Minister has to reshuffle from time to time. It does no harm to throw the occasional man overboard, but it does not do much good if you are steering full steam ahead for the rocks. That is what the Government is now doing' (Holmes 1985, p. 64).

Yet despite such criticism, despite the failures and contradictions, Thatcher's government changed the country's economic/political agenda, and her leading role in this confirmed the power of a determined Prime Minister in economic policy-making. Her conviction and tenacity were critical in changing the economic pattern. She did not do it alone, and similar changes were taking place in other Western states, but it is improbable that the shift would have been as quick or as thorough under a less committed leader. 'What pushed the anti-collectivist counter-revolution so much further in Britain than elsewhere was the historical fluke that the Tory Party had acquired ... a leader of the temper and uncompromising convictions of Margaret Thatcher' (*Contemporary Record* autumn 1987).

10 Foreign Policy

All Prime Ministers have been deeply involved in foreign policy. Most have come to office with direct experience in the field. Four (Eden, Macmillan, Home and Callaghan) had been Foreign Secretaries; Heath had been a Foreign Office minister; and Churchill had been immersed in global affairs throughout his long career. Attlee and Wilson had had narrower experiences, but Attlee had been on the Simon Commission to India in the 1920s, and as Deputy Prime Minister during the war had chaired foreign affairs committees; while Wilson, as President of the Board of Trade in Attlee's government, had a thorough grounding in international economic affairs. Thatcher and Major are exceptions. Major's experience was confined to three uncomfortable months as Foreign Secretary before he returned to the Treasury, and Thatcher had no direct government experience of foreign policy. However, as leader of the opposition she had set out with her usual vigour to make what amends she could by visiting 23 countries in four years.

Even if Prime Ministers were reluctant to involve themselves in foreign policy (and there have been few signs of that) they are drawn in from the obligations of office. As Britain's chief executive, the Prime Minister is the government's principal representative at international gatherings, on overseas tours and when foreign dignitaries visit Britain. The obligations have increased steadily with improved transport and communications and with the proliferation of independent states and international organizations. There have been differences among premiers in the degree of involvement, but it has been substantial in all cases, and all Prime Ministers have chaired the Cabinet's foreign and defence committee. Attlee comes closest to being an exception, because he delegated so much to Ernest Bevin, his Foreign Secretary, but even Attlee was caught in the web of international affairs, as was demonstrated when the day after assuming office in 1945 he flew to Potsdam as leader of the British delegation.

There is therefore obligation, but that has been strongly reinforced by personal inclination. All Prime Ministers want to leave a lasting mark and there is no more tempting prospect than to do so on the broad canvas of international affairs. Attlee took personal charge of arrangements for India's independence: 'His most important contribution to the history of his time' (Harris 1982, p. 362). Churchill, when nearing 80, told the 1953 Tory conference: 'If I stay it is because I have a feeling that I may, through things that have happened, have an influence on what I care about above all else, the building of a lasting and sure peace' (Rhodes James 1986, p. 372). Crossman wrote of Wilson: 'One of the abiding facts about Harold's foreign policy is that he always sees himself as being able to help. He wants to run a foreign policy that enables him to shine as a negotiator, to intervene .... He sees himself influencing events personally' (Crossman 1977, p. 414). Thatcher saw herself playing a crucial part in East/West relations. However, hopes can be dupes. Churchill did not gain the peace summit, nor did Wilson resolve the Rhodesian and Vietnam problems. In the wake of such high expectations bitter disappointment can follow. Following the failure of the 1960 summit, for which Macmillan had worked so hard, he wrote of 'disappointment amounting almost to despair – so much attempted so little achieved' (Macmillan 1972, p. 213).

A further incentive to involvement in foreign affairs is that it can offer political rewards. An overseas tour, or a visit from a foreign leader may give respite from intransigent domestic problems and project the Prime Minister as a statesman standing tall on the world stage above the hurly-burly of domestic conflict. After Macmillan's 1958 Commonwealth tour a newspaper commented: 'Whatever Macmillan may have done for the Commonwealth, the Commonwealth has certainly done something for Macmillan' (Macmillan 1971, p. 410). Foreign visits lend themselves to generous media coverage, and this has increased with television's endless search for pictures: the arrival at the airport, the comings and goings at No. 10, and so on. Thatcher had major television successes when she entertained Presidents Reagan and Gorbachev in Britain, and she had superstar treatment in Moscow in 1987 where she moved easily among the crowds and dominated interviewers. 'When I visited Moscow nine months later,' wrote Hugo Young, 'her performance was still the subject of pleasurable comment' (Young 1989, p. 514). However, there can be political controversy, as in 1985, when Labour accused Thatcher of using an Asian tour to score domestic points by claiming that under the Tories Britain was no longer the sick man of Europe, and that the government had 'seen off' the National Union of Miners. Denis Healey dubbed her 'Rhoda the Rhino' gloating to foreigners about the humiliation of British trade unionists.

Nor has the commitment to foreign policy always been popular with political advisers, because it absorbs time and energy which they believe could be better employed on pressing domestic affairs. Marcia Williams complained about Wilson: 'I had the strong view that the real problems were at home and we needed to concentrate our attention there' (Williams 1972, p. 40). Douglas Hurd, who ironically later became Foreign Secretary, made a similar complaint when he was Heath's adviser. He said that the Prime Minister spent too much time on international affairs, and cited the bitter dispute over the sale of arms to South Africa, which 'bore little relation to the central purpose of Mr Heath's government . . . . The whole issue turned out to be an irrelevance' (Rose and Suleiman 1980, p. 38). The amount of Prime Ministerial time absorbed by foreign policy has not been reduced by quicker transport, for the number and diversity of the contacts have increased and the 'quick dash' visit has become common. In later years it would have been unthinkable to spend days sailing across the Atlantic as Churchill did on his three trips to the US in the 1950s, or to spend six weeks on a Commonwealth tour of Africa as Macmillan did in 1960. Yet there has been no reduction in the time given to foreign visits. In 1988 Thatcher also spent six weeks abroad, but in that time she attended meetings of the EEC, the Group of Ten and the Commonwealth; she visited the US and Poland; and she had an extensive Eastern tour finishing in Australia. By the end of 1988 she had spent nearly a full year of her nine and a half years as Prime Minister on visits abroad.

For most Prime Ministers the longer they stay in office the greater becomes their involvement in foreign policy. There are two main reasons for this. First, with experience a Prime Minister becomes an internationally established figure who understands the style and structure of foreign relations, knows other leaders and becomes increasingly influential. Thatcher exemplified this. From the beginning she gained attention because she was a woman and because of her strong personality, but she was inexperienced and her full impact only came after she had built up the knowledge and contacts which made her a formidable international presence. After ten years in office she had outlasted all other Western leaders and generated respect if not always warmth wherever she went. The second factor is more negative and relates to the scene at home. Usually the longer a government stays in power the more its domestic difficulties increase, as policies fail and problems mount up for which there is no ready solution. In these circumstances there is a temptation for Prime Ministers to turn increasingly to foreign affairs where they escape the immediate pressures, receive deference and are not held directly responsible for all that goes wrong.

Special Concerns

Within the broad range of foreign policy Prime Ministers have characteristically played leading parts in: matters concerning Britain's international status; the development of atomic and nuclear weapons; 'Super Power' relations; and times of crisis.

Britain's international status has been at stake in the ending of the Empire (coupled with the expansion of the Commonwealth), in attempts to retain a global ('Great Power') role and in membership of the EEC. As in other spheres, Prime Ministers have had mixed success. Churchill was a man of Empire who mourned its demise; Eden was sceptical about the EEC; Wilson, although applying for membership of the Community, was more attached to the Commonwealth; and all Prime Ministers (up to Wilson's first period in office) hoped to retain Britain's 'Great Power' status. However, there were positive achievements. As previously noted, Attlee oversaw the independence of India and Pakistan, and later Macmillan accelerated the imperial withdrawal with his 'Wind of Change' speech. As the Empire withered, Prime Ministers were prominent in trying to build a new Commonwealth, and, when that faltered, in leading the country towards the EEC, unsuccessfully for Macmillan and Wilson but triumphantly for Heath. Even after EEC entry, Wilson, Callaghan and above all Thatcher led vigorous campaigns to counter the challenge to Britain's sovereignty from Brussels.

Membership of the EEC brought extensive new obligations. The scope and workings of the Community are so broad that they stretch across any dividing line that might be drawn between 'domestic' and 'foreign' affairs to produce a new constitutional position whereby Britain, like other members, is 'condemned to agree' on a wide range of topics. But reaching agreement requires intensive and sustained negotiation in which most ministers, not least the Prime Minister, are regularly involved. For the Prime Minister a series of new commitments has arisen in working with European partners: to implement what the Community has already agreed, to probe areas in which fresh agreements are sought, to hammer out common responses to international developments and to explain and reconcile Community developments to British interests. Major finds himself working with other member governments and the Commission in Brussels in a way that would have astonished Prime Ministers of the 1950s. EEC affairs consume much of his time and energy – in formal meetings and in managing

Community relations at home and abroad. That situation had not come easily to Thatcher. The relationship with the Community was a divisive issue within her government, creating rifts between her and some of her most senior colleagues. In his resignation speech Geoffrey Howe accused her of conjuring up a nightmare of a Community 'positively teeming with ill-intentioned people, scheming, in her words, "to extinguish democracy", to dissolve our national identity.' 'What kind of vision is that?' he asked, and he concluded that 'her attitude towards Europe is running increasingly serious risks for the future of our nation.' Yet, despite her doubts and her instinctive suspicion, Thatcher realized that Britain's interests were served by working within the Community and she gave much time and energy in trying to reshape it to her own views, and to ensuring that British interests were protected.

Prime Ministers have taken personal responsibility for decisions on atomic and nuclear weapons. When development of the atomic bomb started during the war Churchill kept it secret from most ministers (including Attlee and other Labour leaders). Attlee later behaved in the same way, by excluding the full Cabinet, using a small *ad hoc* group of ministers, officials and services chiefs and ensuring that 'no major decisions ... were taken without his prior approval' (Gowing 1974, p. 27). In six years Attlee only raised the matter ten times in Cabinet and then mainly to give information. Churchill, in his peace-time ministry, was at first an exception because he consulted the full Cabinet: 'The first and last time that a British cabinet has been allowed to take the decision on a new generation of nuclear weapons' (Hennessy 1986, p. 135). However, later he decided not to tell ministers about the development of the hydrogen bomb which he discussed personally with President Eisenhower. Eden and Macmillan followed similar paths, and it was by personal negotiation with President Kennedy that Macmillan succeeded in acquiring Polaris.

Wilson and Callaghan had the problem of leading a party with a strong anti-nuclear section. They overcame this first by keeping decisions in the hands of a small group of like-minded ministers, and second by 'bouncing' the Cabinet through claims that the costs of new developments were small or those of cancelling agreements were too high to contemplate. For example, in 1974 Wilson brought to the Cabinet a proposal for a new Polaris development called 'Chevaline'. He introduced it as 'a little bit of modernization' and said that the cost was estimated at £24 m. It went through with little comment and never returned to the Cabinet. Yet, before Wilson left office it had cost almost £600 m. and was continued under Callaghan, who kept it to a small group of ministers and officials; eventually it cost more than £1000 m. Commenting on the broad scene, Callaghan wrote: 'It has always been the role of the Prime Minister of the day to take the lead in discussing nuclear matters with the President of the United States,' and while it was wise to let the Cabinet take decisions on secondary matters, no Prime Minister 'can abdicate his overriding responsibility to safeguard national security, and once his mind is made upon the best course for the country, he must do what he believes is necessary, fight for his decision, and if he cannot get support he should stand down' (Callaghan 1987, p. 558).

Relations with the Super Powers have also attracted the attention of Prime Ministers. At first this was linked to the ambition for Great Power status, but even when that faded personal diplomacy continued in this field. With the possible exceptions of Eden and Heath, the chief aim has been to foster the 'special relationship' with the US, and there have been notable successes. Churchill, who made three visits to the US as Prime Minister, was held in great respect and was able to build on his wartime friendship with President Eisenhower. Relations between Macmillan and Kennedy were so cordial that Macmillan's visits to Washington were 'like a house party and at times almost like a spree' (Horne 1989, pp. 304–5). Even that was overshadowed by the admiration Thatcher and Reagan felt for each other as they established the closest relationship of all. Such contacts are more than socially satisfying, for they have helped to coordinate policy and have brought Britain 'know how', advanced technology (especially in nuclear arms), economic support and shared intelligence. The importance of shared intelligence was amply demonstrated during the Falklands campaign. However, relations have not always been smooth. There were differences in Attlee's day over Palestine; a fierce clash of views at the time of Suez; and, despite his best efforts, Wilson had an uneasy relationship with Lyndon Johnson. Johnson was angry at Wilson's refusal to send British troops to support the US in Vietnam, but George Brown, no lover of Wilson, added, 'I think the fact of the matter was that Mr Johnson didn't really like the Prime Minister much' (Brown 1971, p. 146).

Contacts with the USSR have been sparser, but again personal diplomacy by Prime Ministers has been prominent, as reflected in the efforts of Churchill and Macmillan to organize summits. Macmillan, Wilson, and Thatcher paid visits to the USSR, and visits from Soviet leaders started with Bulganin's and Kruschev's controversial trip during Eden's premiership. The most successful links were established between Thatcher and Gorbachev, as the Soviet leader sought her support as a leading Western figure for glasnost.

As in domestic affairs, Prime Ministers have taken the lead, or been obliged to take the lead in crises. These have included Suez (1956), Rhodesia (1965), the Falklands (1982) and the Gulf (1990/1). Such situations expose leaders to high risks (as Eden discovered when he was broken by Suez) but they can also offer high rewards (as Thatcher demonstrated in her gains from the Falklands campaign). Prime Ministers are aware of this. Crossman wrote that Wilson saw the Rhodesian crisis as 'his Cuba', in which he could make his mark as a world statesman, but he also knew that if he mishandled it the Commonwealth could break up, and at home his government could fall. 'Indeed,' wrote Crossman, 'I think his thoughts have been largely dominated by the determination not to leave his flank open to Heath' (Crossman 1975, p. 377–8).

The Foreign Secretary and the Foreign and Commonwealth Office (FCO)

As with economic policy, the Prime Minister's prominent role can lead to strained relations inside the government, in this case with the Foreign Secretary and the FCO. Sometimes

Foreign Secretaries choose themselves. Eden was so experienced in the field, so senior in the party and so determined to do the job that Churchill, although suggesting that Eden should gain domestic experience, was obliged to have him. Heath was in a similar position when Alec Douglas-Home (exceptionally for an ex-Prime Minister) agreed to serve in the government, and Major was more or less obliged to confirm Douglas Hurd's position in 1990 after defeating him in the leadership role.

More usually, however, the appointments indicate the Prime Minister's own preferred role in foreign affairs. At one extreme Attlee gave Bevin his head on the basis that 'You don't keep a dog and bark yourself — and Ernie was a very good dog' (Bullock 1983, p. 74). Also Wilson, in his second period in office, left much to the experienced Callaghan. He gave the Foreign Secretary a free hand on Europe and Callaghan wrote of a 'cordial' relationship, 'a partnership that was of great value in conducting the Government's affairs' (Callaghan 1987, p. 300). At the other extreme, Eden replaced Macmillan after less than a year because Macmillan was too strong a character and brought in the more compliant Selwyn Lloyd, who, according to one of his officials, acted 'like an office boy' (Shuckburgh 1986, p. 317). When Macmillan himself became Prime Minister he retained Lloyd at the Foreign Office. 'The truth, though he would not admit it,' wrote Alistair Horne, 'was that Macmillan — the frustrated Foreign Secretary (and just like Eden) — wanted to continue to run British foreign policy himself' (Horne 1989, p. 8).

In terms of personal relations some combinations (like Attlee and Bevin, and Wilson and Callaghan) have been both harmonious and balanced in sharing responsibility, but others have been tense. Although Churchill and Eden largely shared each others' views on policy, the relationship was soured by Churchill's reluctance to resign the premiership in Eden's favour. When differences did arise they were exacerbated by personal bitterness, as in the clash over the withdrawal of British troops from the Suez Canal Zone in 1953. Churchill, who wanted to keep them in the Zone, accused Eden of appeasement. 'I never knew', he said, 'that Munich was situated on the Nile' (Gilbert 1988, p. 795). Wilson and Brown also had fierce quarrels, and Brown accused Wilson of plotting behind his back in a dispute over arms sales to South Africa. Thatcher, never, one for mincing words, accused Francis Pym of being a 'quitter' during the Falklands campaign. 'She thinks nothing of him whatever,' said one of her supporters (Young 1989, p. 272). Later she disagreed with Geoffrey Howe over European policy and moved him from the Foreign Office in 1989 without warning.

The Prime Minister's relations with the FCO are not dissimilar from those with the Treasury. Often there is harmony and the FCO's advice is sought and respected. Among others, Eden, Home, Macmillan and Wilson praised the devotion and quality of the department, but the potential for tension is inherent because No. 10 and the FCO operate in the same field but with different time scales, different constituencies and different styles. The FCO has to react to and keep contact with other governments and international organizations while seeking to advance British interests. That carries the danger that the FCO will pay too little attention to domestic politics and too much to external views. In the blunt terms of a conviction politician like Thatcher it makes them 'wet', and Norman Tebbit probably reflected her view when he concluded that 'The Ministry of Agriculture looks after farmers; the Foreign Office after foreigners' (Cosgrave 1985, p. 113). The FCO is a bureaucracy pursuing international relations through established norms and practices, committed to diplomacy and often working to long time horizons. Prime Ministers are politicians with shorter time scales, eager to solve particular problems by personal contacts.

The enthusiasm of Prime Ministers for summit meetings underlines the point. Churchill did not believe that 'endless discussions between Foreign Offices (could) produce any decisive results' (Gilbert 1988, p. 1039). He wanted direct personal negotiations. In 1953 he proposed a summit that was informal and private and not overwhelmed by 'a ponderous or rigid agenda, or lead into mazes and jungles of technical details, zealously constructed by hoards of experts and officials'. In contrast, Eden, who as Foreign Secretary reflected the Foreign Office view, was opposed to meetings of 'the mighty few', with no agenda, and no preparation, and instead favoured careful preparation and expert advice (Rhodes James 1986, p. 365). Yet, when Eden became Prime Minister he was quickly bitten by the summit bug and vigorously set out to organize one in 1955. From retirement Churchill wryly commented: 'How much more attractive a top level meeting seems when one has reached the top' (Carlton 1981, p. 372).

From time to time Prime Ministers have short-circuited the FCO by using their own lines of advice and communication and their own advisers. For example, Sir Harold Cassia, the British Ambassador in Washington, sent direct personal telegrams to Macmillan. In September 1957 he alerted the Prime Minister to possible US action in Syria without going through the Foreign Office. In that case not only did Macmillan have a direct personal line but he confided in his diary 'the responsibility cannot really be shared with the Cabinet' (Horne 1989, p. 43). Marcia Williams wrote of a gulf between Wilson and the FCO in relations with Israel. She claimed that because Wilson was a strong Israeli supporter, while the FCO was sympathetic to the Arabs, the officials often failed to keep him informed of what was happening, including what line the British UN representatives were taking. Therefore No. 10's political office (Donoughue, Haines and Williams) acted 'as go-between outside the official channels'. She cited an incident in 1975 when Wilson while visiting Helsinki alerted Israel to a change in US policy. As he could not trust the FCO, he telephoned Williams and, using a veiled message (presumably fearing his line was 'bugged'), arranged for the Israelis to contact him directly (Falkender 1983, pp. 157, 177).

Prime Ministers also look to advice from other departments of government, partly because of the overlap between foreign and domestic policies, and partly to gain alternative views. Many departments are drawn into EEC affairs, and the secret intelligence service (MI6) provides an alternative source of information on international concerns which the Prime Minister can tap directly. Premiers also use individual advisers. In

Thatcher's case she appointed Sir Anthony Parsons to No. 10, on the basis of his performance at the UN during the Falklands war and in the belief that he was not 'one of them', and when Sir Anthony retired she replaced him with Sir Philip Craddick. Prime Ministers can also draw on the private secretaries who are seconded from the FCO, and in some cases have relied heavily on them, as noted earlier in the case of Philip Zulueta and Charles Powell.

11 The Power of Prime Minister

There is a long-running debate about the power of the Prime Minister. This was particularly active in the 1960s and 1970s when three broad interpretations emerged: the presidential; the chairmanship; and personality/circumstances.

The presidential approach sets the Prime Minister on a pinnacle of power, above and apart from ministerial colleagues. Richard Crossman championed this view in his 1964 introduction to Walter Bagehot's *The English Constitution*, when he stated that 'the post-war epoch has seen the final transformation of Cabinet Government into Prime Ministerial Government.' After outlining the range of powers at the Prime Minister's disposal — the selection and dismissal of ministers, the control of Cabinet business, the leadership of the ruling party and the control of key civil service posts — Crossman concluded that the premier had replaced the Cabinet as the major coordinating force in government. He argued that increased government activity had led to greater centralization, so that decisions were no longer taken by the Cabinet as a body, but by the separate departments and Cabinet committees interacting with the Prime Minister, who, in any case, had appointed them. The result was that the doctrine of collective responsibility now 'means collective obedience by the whole administration . . . to the will of the man at the apex of power'. Furthermore, Crossman argued that parliament was no longer a body of independently minded men acting as a check on the executive but a body run by party machines in which the Prime Minister controlled the ruling group (Crossman 1963).

Crossman re-examined the position some years later after serving in Wilson's Cabinet, an experience which entrenched his views. Although he accepted that by mismanagement or lack of success a Prime Minister could undermine his own position, and that ultimately the Cabinet retained reserve powers which could reduce the premier to *primus inter pares*, these only applied in the most unusual circumstances. If, Crossman argued, a Prime Minister decided to play a chairmanship role it was because he had chosen not to use powers which belonged to the office. He cited Attlee as an example, and also mentioned Eden giving way to Macmillan, after Macmillan, as Chancellor, had threatened to resign. According to Crossman, 'the moral of the story is not that a Prime Minister is not empowered to give orders to a Chancellor, but on that occasion Mr Eden did not dare to use the power he undoubtedly possesses.' Further, although Crossman recognized that Prime Ministers had to bear in mind party considerations (potential rivals and the need for support in parliament), this was more than countered by their control of government business and patronage, because all who accepted posts, whether inside or outside the Cabinet, were bound to the government by 'collective responsibility'. In addition Prime Ministers controlled senior civil service appointments, and thereby gained deference from the senior mandarins beyond that accorded to other ministers. Crossman's conclusion was that power was concentrated in the Prime Minister who stood on the pinnacles of the government's political and administrative structures (Crossman 1972).

Crossman was not alone in his views. Among others he was joined by Tony Benn who served in Labour Cabinets under Wilson and Callaghan. Benn concluded that Britain now had an 'Absolute Premiership' in which power was so centralized that government decisions had become the personal views of the Prime Minister rather than the collective views of the ministers. He wrote of a 'system of personal rule in the very heart of our Parliamentary democracy'. Benn argued:

That the wide range of powers at present exercised by a British Prime Minister, both in that capacity, and as Party Leader, are now so great as to encroach upon the legitimate rights of the electorate, undermine the essential role of Parliament, usurp some of the functions of collective cabinet decision making, and neutralise much of the influence deriving from the internal democracy of the Party. (Benn 1979)

The presidential view did not go unchallenged. In 1965 G. W. Jones argued that the premier's position is best understood as that of a chairman who is subject to constraints and dependent on the support of others. Jones was not arguing that Prime Ministers are powerless but that they are leaders of a group (the Cabinet) rather than figures set apart, and the group, far from being subservient, is composed of powerful political figures and potential rivals. In choosing a Cabinet a Prime Minister does not have a free hand but has to satisfy the diverse interests and personalities within the party and has often to give office to those who have different views. 'There is no loyalty at the top because the Prime Minister's colleagues are his rivals, eager to replace him, and he is engaged in a constant battle to fend them off' (King 1969, p. 205).

Jones further argued that to remain in office the Prime Minister must carry his colleagues with him, wooing and coaxing them in a continuing dialogue in which it would be fatal to be isolated from supporters inside and outside parliament. Nor, Jones said, are ministers and MPs rubber stamps because the Prime Minister depends on their support and therefore must accommodate their views. Therefore 'collective responsibility' does not imply obedience to the premier but rather reaching agreed positions which all (including the Prime Minister) have to accept. The constraints extend to policy-making where the huge scope of government business means that Prime Ministers can only be involved in a small part of it, and even when they do participate they have to contend with department interests and expertise. Jones drew a similar picture in the conduct of Cabinet business. Prime Ministers may be able to delay consideration of an item but not for long if colleagues are determined to discuss it, and in summarizing Cabinet discussions they cannot go against the sense of the meeting. They must retain the Cabinet's confidence which means they cannot dictate to it. Jones concluded that 'A Prime Minister who can carry his colleagues with him can be in a very powerful position, but he is only as strong as they let him be' (King 1969, p. 216).

Similar conclusions were reached by Patrick Cosgrave in 1972 when he argued that 'it is difficult for Prime Ministers to achieve their ends because it has rarely been possible for any Prime Minister to exercise that broad, continuous and effective and successful implementation of desired reform.' Cosgrave wrote of the punishing routine of office which exhausts even the most active of leaders, and, rather than calling for a reduction of powers, he called for a strengthening of the Prime Minister's Office in relation to departments (Cosgrave 1972). In the same vein Douglas Jay, looking back on his time as Attlee's parliamentary private secretary, disputed the claim that great power lay with the Prime Minister, and instead emphasized the constraints that surround the office. Jay challenged the picture of a Prime Minister 'sitting down in his office, pulling great levers, issuing edicts, and shaping events. Nothing could be further from the truth in the real life of No. 10 as I knew it' (Jay 1980).

The 'chairmanship' approach also gained considerable if not unqualified support from Jock Bruce-Gardyne and Nigel Lawson who examined a number of government decisions during the 1960s: the building of Concorde, the abortive approaches to the EEC in 1961 and 1967, the abolition of the resale price maintenance in 1963/4 and the decisions not to devalue the pound between 1964 and 1967. They concluded that the presidential approach did not stand up well, for in these cases it was only the 'non-decision' about devaluation which was truly dominated by the Prime Minister (Wilson). They concluded that usually Prime Ministers alone could not carry the day but they did exercise a critical role in tipping the balance when there was uncertainty or division. As examples they argued that Macmillan's support clinched the decision over Concorde, and, similarly, that the application for EEC membership in 1967 would not have gone forward, despite the enthusiasm of ministers like Brown and Jenkins, had not Wilson been converted. They drew a picture of the premier 'as an arbiter of choice in government, rather than a preselector of decisions' whose acquiescence is necessary for major policy decisions 'even if that acquiescence has sometimes to be extracted by something akin to "force majeure." '. They argued that a strong Prime Minister is not indispensable for decisive government, citing the examples of activity continuing unabated under Home, and Wilson's more relaxed style in his second term being more effective than the frantic activity of the first (Bruce-Gardyne and Lawson 1976).

In advancing their views, neither the advocates of the presidential nor of the chairmanship interpretations placed great emphasis on the personalities of Prime Ministers or the circumstances they face. They built their cases on the broad developments of the office. They were more concerned with 'the office' than 'the individual', with 'processes' rather than 'circumstances'. Yet for others, personality and circumstance are central to understanding. Lord Asquith, the Liberal Prime Minister in the early part of the century, claimed that 'the office of Prime Minister is what the holder chooses and is able to make of it.' Among others, Lord Blake has shared this view. He wrote of the need for a Prime Ministerial temperament, which is difficult to define, but Blake included 'courage, tenacity, determination, firm nerves, ... clarity of mind, toughness of skin and lack of great sensitivity', while tact and the ability to manage men are valuable additions. Blake argued that 'possession of the right temperament is not a guarantee of success but lack of it is a guarantee of failure.' There were other personal characteristics that Blake thought were important. He did not believe that Prime Ministers need have original minds, although Lloyd George and Churchill showed those qualities as war leaders, but in less critical times Blake supported a view attributed to Peel that a Prime Minister should be 'a man of common opinion and uncommon abilities'.

Blake did not lay the full burden of explanation on personality, but added both the different circumstances faced by Prime Ministers and institutional developments. Prime Ministers are not able to dictate the changes and chances that surround their governments and they may be more or less fortunate in those that arise. In that he was supported by Bruce-Gardyne and Lawson who also noted the importance of changing circumstances, the shifting scene, in which a premier's fortunes could rise and fall depending on the government's standing in the country. They concluded that so long as a premier can deliver the electoral goods his power, uninhibited by a written constitution, may be greater than that of a president elsewhere, but if the government ran into serious electoral trouble the Prime Minister's position became much weaker. On his part Blake emphasized that Prime Ministers cannot dictate the changes and chances, but the element of fortune also tests the ability and personality of Prime Ministers to respond to challenges. Furthermore, extraordinary circumstances produce extraordinary personalities, as in the cases of Lloyd George and Churchill who gained the premiership in wartime, whereas in more settled times these ebullient characters may have been kept in the wings.

In terms of institutional developments, Blake argued that these were not as dramatic as Crossman had suggested. He accused Crossman of lacking historical perspective, for premiers of earlier times had exercised great powers and none had come nearer to presidential-like behaviour than Lloyd George, who held office before the features of government appeared which Crossman claimed had so enhanced the premier's powers. For Blake, the significance of institutional developments was that they created the framework for the interplay of personality and circumstance. 'The truth is', he wrote, 'that the powers of the Prime Minister have varied with the personality of the Prime Minister, or with the particular political circumstances of his tenure.' In terms of relationship within government the balance has only altered slowly and over long periods. 'The differences, if we are to take any half century, or even more, are largely between personalities − the way in which this or that occupant of 10 Downing Street in the light of his own circumstances feels he should or can or wants to behave' (Blake 1975).

The Thatcher Factor

The debate outlined above took place before Thatcher's remarkable tenure in office. It was remarkable in a number of ways: she was the first woman to hold the office, she held power much longer than any other Prime Minister this century and she had an unusual sense of conviction and a personal policy agenda which did not always coincide with that of the rest of her government. The 'presidential' and 'personality' schools were quick to claim her as their own, depending on whether they favour a general trend explanation (i.e. towards presidential government) or the shifting pattern of personality and circumstances. The 'presidential' saw her continuing along a path already stamped out by her predecessors of increasingly centralized decision-making. The 'personality' school emphasized her dominant and distinctive character, and the way in which through hard work and force of personality she imposed her will on the government.

Both schools can find ample evidence. For example, they could both, in their different ways, point to Thatcher's performance at the Conservative Women's conference in June 1990. Senior colleagues had been counselling caution because of the government's poor standing in opinion polls. Thatcher would have none of it. 'We will never run out of steam,' she told the conference. 'Like climbing a hill, you think you are near the top and then you see another peak beyond'. Without having consulted her ministers, she then outlined a personal manifesto – including new proposals for privately funded lorry motorway lanes, for schools dropping out of local authority control and for coping with family problems caused by the high divorce rate. One cabinet minister spoke of her 'shooting from the hip' (*Independent* 25 June 1990).

The 'chairmanship' school had a more difficult task. Thatcher's public image, and indeed her own self-perception, did not easily fit the model of a chairman collecting colleagues' views, seeking compromises and balancing contending parties. Rather she was seen as a dominant figure drawing power into her own hands, imposing her convictions on others, riding roughshod over opponents, reducing the role of the Cabinet and giving less attention to parliament than her predecessors. Few Prime Ministers have generated so much controversy, so much love and hate, and the media revelled in 'the iron lady', she who is 'not for turning', and 'Attila the hen'.

However, G. H. Jones challenged the predominant views with a modified version of his earlier 'chairmanship' approach. The modification was the greater attention he paid to personality and circumstance. Writing in 1990, he pointed out that accusations of being autocratic had not been confined to Thatcher, and again he stressed the constraints surrounding the premier. The office of Prime Minister, like the Cabinet is a convention, and 'as a convention the office is like an elastic band. It can be stretched to accommodate an assertive Prime Minister and contracted for a Prime Minister with a more relaxed style.' He suggested that four factors come into play: the premier's own concept of the office; what other ministers are prepared to tolerate; the issues that are under consideration; and the current popularity of the Prime Minister and the government. Jones argued that since Thatcher came to power there had been a flow backwards and forwards between periods of dominance and vulnerability. He cited 1989, a year which 'saw the Prime Minister's power raised up and dashed down'. In May she had celebrated ten years in power with her government strong and her personal standing high, but by the end of the year she and her government were deep in troubles and she was 'embattled, trapped in a more assertive cabinet, unable to rely on her backbenchers and fighting for survival'.

On more general issues Jones stated that Thatcher's use of Cabinet committees and bilateral meetings with ministers was more likely to constrain than strengthen her personal power because , had she turned to the full Cabinet, she could have appealed to less informed ministers who were dependent on her patronage. Also, like previous Prime Ministers, she had acted as guardian of the collective Cabinet against the danger of rampant departmentalism. Then, paying respect to personality, Jones said that while some Prime Ministers were content to act as chairmen, others, like Thatcher, had injected their own sense of mission into government, but how far they can go depends on the attitude of colleagues. 'If a Prime Minister is "too powerful," it is because ministers have allowed her to become so. She is only as powerful as they let her be.' Added to that are the interplay of issues, in which the premier is more vulnerable if there is a party split or if public popularity falls. Jones concluded that 'Mrs Thatcher has not changed the office of Prime Minister ... . She has stretched the elastic. Her dominance is not structural, but political and contingent, dependent on her will, the response of her ministerial colleagues, the issues under consideration and the standing of the government at a particular moment' (*Contemporary Record* April 1990).

Jones could soon claim that his views had been justified when Thatcher fell from office seven months after the article was published. Among the factors he had identified he could point to the unpopularity of the government and the Prime Minister (as measured by opinion polls) that had caused such disquiet among Tories and created a setting for the leadership challenge. He could also point to the limits of ministerial tolerance. That was revealed most obviously by Howe's resignation but also by the reaction of other ministers during the leadership contest. After the first indecisive round, in which Thatcher had received the support of her ministerial colleagues, she declared that 'I fight on; I fight to win.' She then set about rallying the faint-hearted in the Cabinet by calling them individually to No. 10. Far from receiving a renewed vote of confidence she found that most of the Cabinet thought that her support was slipping and some said openly that she should resign. It was that which determined her decision to go. A Prime Minister who had been so dominant and was so keen to continue could not survive without the support of her colleagues.

Fluctuating Powers

The debate on the Prime Minister's power continues and will continue because no absolute conclusions can be drawn. The available evidence is always partial, open to different interpretations and subject to normative judgements (what we believe 'ought to be'). The bold lines of the debate between the advocates of the presidential and chairmanship approaches have advantages, but such approaches can undervalue the shifting pattern of behaviour and the ups and downs of political life, not just between different Prime Ministers but in the experience of each Prime Minister. Three main factors are involved: first the constitutional and political frameworks in which Prime Ministers operate; second, the circumstances that they face; and third, their personality and personal qualities.

The constitutional and political frameworks are built on precedent and convention. Lord Blake was right to emphasize that these only change slowly, and Jones' analogy of the elastic band is helpful in underlining that the frameworks have flexibility but also exercise constraints on Prime Ministers. As noted earlier, there have been changes in constitutional and political practice since 1945, for example in the pattern of Cabinet meetings and the election of party leaders, but they have been amendments to the existing structures rather than new structures. For example, there is no Prime Minister's Department and Prime Ministers still have to work within the context created by Cabinet and parliamentary government.

In contrast with the constitutional and political frameworks, the second factor, the circumstances that face a Prime Minister, are constantly changing and are unpredictable. A Prime Minister may or may not inherit a difficult political situation, or have to contend with an international crisis or a major change in the international economy. Macmillan's early years, for example, coincided with a general growth in the international economy, whereas Heath had to face the oil crisis of 1973/4. For much of her premiership Thatcher enjoyed the good fortune of facing weak political opposition. The Labour Party was passing through troubled times, and to add to that the opposition was divided between Labour and the Alliance. In that sense luck comes into the calculation of a Prime Minister's power, but so does his/her capacity to counter bad fortune and take maximum advantage of good fortune. Successful politicians are opportunists.

Major demonstrated that vital combination of luck and

opportunism in gaining the premiership. He was lucky in the way the leadership contest developed. The challenge to Thatcher was created by Howe's resignation and Heseltine's bid for office, while Major played the loyal lieutenant, being one of Thatcher's nominators. When Thatcher stood down the whole scene changed. Now there was both a guilt factor and a loyalty factor in Tory behaviour: a guilt factor in having forced Thatcher out; a loyalty factor in wanting to rally the party together, to demonstrate to Thatcher that her achievements were fully appreciated, and bitterness among some members towards Heseltine. The opportunism came in the way Major exploited the situation. At first there seemed no reason why the Tories should not turn to Douglas Hurd, a more experienced minister and a more establishment figure than Major, but Major and his supporters, through an efficient and dynamic campaign, rapidly created a momentum, a sense that he would be the winner, that his was the bandwagon on which to climb, and to crown his efforts the guilt and loyalty factors came further into play when Thatcher let it be known that 'John was her boy.'

The third factor, the personal qualities, vary markedly between Prime Ministers but are reasonably fixed in the case of an individual. Prime Ministers develop with experience and may in time, as in Wilson's case, produce a different style of premiership, but personalities are largely shaped before they reach No. 10 and the question is how they use their individual talents in the post. To an extent Prime Ministers make their own luck. Thatcher handled the Falklands crisis more effectively than Eden handled Suez and deservedly gained political credit from it, but later when she failed to listen to the warnings about the poll tax she lost political capital and was forced to modify her position in the face of criticism in parliament and the party and from local governments. One way of comparing Prime Ministers would be to make a check list of the personal resources they have brought to office and then judge how well they have used those resources: such as ability to work hard; to identify clear aims; to take quick decisions; to compromise; to innovate; to choose able subordinates; to delegate successfully; to generate enthusiasm and respect; to handle opposition both inside and outside the government; and to communicate effectively with colleagues and the public.

By putting the three factors together − constitutional and political frameworks, circumstance and personality − the picture that emerges is one of fluctuating powers, whereby at some times a Prime Minister may appear to have a presidential-like position, whereas at others he/she is subject to obvious constraints. For example, the Prime Minister's strength was demonstrated in July 1965 when Crossman, who was then Minister of Housing, was called before a committee of five of his Cabinet colleagues responsible for examining and reporting on government cuts. Crossman knew that he had Harold Wilson's sympathy and support. After an hour-long argument Crossman recorded:

> Douglas Houghton said: 'I must say I don't like this at all. The others all came in here fearing their programmes will be cut. This fellow saunters into the room giving the impression that we dare not cut him for political reasons.' Of course, what Houghton said was the precise truth. I know I have the Prime Minister behind me. (Crossman 1975, p. 268)

In that instance Crossman was demonstrating the Prime Minister's power. In contrast, another example drawn from that same month illustrates the limitation of that power. Again, public expenditure was involved, and on this occasion both James Callaghan, as Chancellor, and George Brown, as Secretary of State for Economic Affairs, combined against Wilson to prevent the restoration of £20 m. from cuts in the overseas aid budget, although Barbara Castle, the Minister of Overseas Development, had gained Wilson's support in attempting to restore the cuts. On previous occasions when Callaghan and Brown had opposed each other the Prime Minister's support had been decisive because he held the balance, but in this case when the two major 'economic ministers' were united, their combined weight left Wilson with no presidential-like powers. When Wilson showed sympathy for Barbara Castle, a long argument ensued:

> The First Secretary and the Chancellor, clearly in some sense

working together, leapt on Harold like wolfhounds in at the kill
. . . . They tore him from both sides. They insulted him, tried
to pull him down in the most violent way, obviously both feeling
that Harold was evading his responsibilities as Prime Minister
and trying to do an unseemly fix. And of course that is what he
was doing . . . . When he was defeated he tried to pretend he
hadn't made the proposal. (Crossman 1975, p. 282)

The Power to Achieve Goals

So far the discussion of the Prime Minister's power has been
about relationships in government – whether, for example, the
premier does or does not dominate Cabinet colleagues, and
whether he/she chooses to use one set of advisers rather than
another. 'Power' in that sense is the ability to influence others,
not the identification and implementation of goals. However,
power can also be seen in terms of goal seeking – of what
premiers have set out to achieve and what they have achieved.
Judged in that light some Prime Ministers have concentrated
less on policies and more on holding the party and government
together to face the unforeseen problems and circumstances
that always arise. Among these were Home, who had little
choice because of his difficult inheritance, and Wilson (accused
by critics of having no policy objectives) who made clear his
intention of making the Labour Party the natural party of
government. Most Prime Ministers, however, have a range of
aims, which will include consolidating their party's hold on
power and achieving policy goals.

There are problems in assessing policy goal achievement.
First, the goals are usually vague, such as the maintenance of
order and the restoration of full employment. Second, they are
usually shared by, or a product of the ruling party and the
government, and not distinctive to the premier. It is difficult
therefore to distinguish between the premier's goals and
achievements and those of the government as a whole. Again,
Thatcher is an exception. As Anthony King wrote: 'She is
probably unique among 20th-century Prime Ministers in having

a policy agenda – a set of views and a set of priorities – that is peculiarly her own and is in no way merely an emanation of her government and party' (King 1985, p. 98). It might also be argued that as leaders all Prime Ministers, including Thatcher, have to bear responsibility for whatever their governments do. A third problem is that fortunes vary over time. Turning again to King, he said that Thatcher's first administration could be divided into three distinct periods. In the first (May 1979 to autumn 1981) things went badly wrong, the economy was in great trouble and the Cabinet deeply divided, a period that Thatcher 'would probably prefer to forget'. Then from the autumn 1981 to April 1982 matters started to improve: public spending and inflation were brought down, and inside the government Thatcher gained ground by removing some opponents and winning more arguments. The civil war was over, an uneasy compromise reigned, but the Prime Minister was 'still on trial'. In the third period Thatcher enjoyed great success, partly because the economic picture continued to improve but mainly because of the Falklands war which Thatcher handled with such determination, reflecting the national mood. After that 'her position of overall dominance was never again in doubt' (King 1985, pp. 101–7). If such ups and downs (periods when the premier and the government could be judged a success at one time a failure at another) could be identified in her first administration how much more could they be seen in the years that followed?

Because of the difficulties it is probably only in retrospect that overall judgements can be made about goal achievements. The one government in post-war years that is usually given credit for achieving most of its goals is Attlee's. Yet even in that case controversy continues, not least about Attlee's own contribution; for some he is the guiding hand who deserves the greatest credit, for others he is a mouse who was fortunate to be surrounded by able colleagues who drove the government forward. As for other administrations, the judgements are more often than not of under-achievement and even failure. Economic performance is often cited as an example where government after government has promised but failed to match the per-

formance of the more succesful Western economies. The result
is that many Prime Ministers have been disappointed. Writing
in 1981, James Margach said that in the twentieth century few
had left office 'as happy, contented, and fulfilled men' (Margach
1981, p. 39).

What explains the gap between goal aims and achievements?
One possibility is that the gap seems wider than it is because
the media, political opponents and critics emphasize failures,
not achievements — the old story that good news is no news.
At the 1976 Labour conference Callaghan turned on those
who claimed that his government had failed to implement the
party manifesto. 'The remarkable thing is', he said, 'not what
we have failed to do but how much we have carried out,' and
he said that many of the aims of the Labour pioneers were now
in the statute book (Callaghan 1987, p. 94). Another reason for
the gap, especially in Prime Ministers' performance, is that
they are drawn into the most intractable and sensitive problems.
There is great appeal in a Prime Minister pursuing a major
challenge. Who can resist the scene in 1868 when Gladstone,
on receiving news that he was to form another ministry, paused
from felling a tree on his estate in North Wales to declare: 'My
mission is to pacify Ireland'? A splendid scene, an admirable
objective, but neither he nor any of his successors have achieved
that mission. In post-war years the Irish problem has flared up
again and again, to stand alongside economic growth, industrial
relations, Britain's place in the EEC, and so on, as matters on
which all Prime Ministers and governments have positions but
limited ability to achieve their ends.

In such cases Prime Ministers and government may be
adding to their own burdens by making unrealizable claims.
Wilson, for example, has been accused of cultivating a public
image 'that the powers of government to change men and
especially their economic destiny was boundless' (Walker in
Hennessy and Seldon 1987, p. 192). There may also be contradictions in the government's aims. One of Thatcher's stated
aims was to roll back the frontiers of government and yet many
of her radical goals could only be achieved by government
interference, by more, not less, involvement. Finally there are

circumstances which arise which are outside the control of the premier or the government. Crossman recorded in his diary that while Wilson was able to bluff his way past fellow ministers he could not overcome 'economic forces' at home and abroad that were holding back the government. Similarly in 1976 Callaghan's government faced such bleak international and domestic circumstances that it was forced to turn for help to the IMF, despite the reluctance of many ministers.

For all the problems and uncertainties surrounding judgements about goal achievement Prime Ministers and governments are not powerless in this respect. That was not so clear in 1979. Callaghan's government had overcome the immediate crisis of 1976 but when it fell in 1979 there was speculation that Britain had become 'ungovernable': that a combination of corporate interests, economic problems and the mood of the times made it impossible for the government to set its own aims. The view was advanced that the government could be little more than a referee, and not a particularly effective one, between the competing interests. Thatcher changed that. She showed that by determination, conviction, luck and bullying a Prime Minister could not only set objectives but achieve some of them. She failed to gain many of her goals, and some she did gain were deeply unpopular, but not only did she pursue an agenda, she succeeded in changing the political climate and generating a new mood within the country — albeit one that incorporated increased political bitterness. She demonstrated that, despite all problems and constraints, a determined Prime Minister can set out to achieve goals, and that Britain is 'governable'.

Bibliography

Beloff, N. (1973) *Transit of Britain* (Collins).

Benn, A. (1979) *The Case for a Constitutional Premiership* (Institute for Workers' Control).

Blake, R. (1975) *The Office of Prime Minister* (Oxford University Press).

Brown, G. (1971) *In My Way* (Victor Gollancz).

Bruce-Gardyne, J. and Lawson, N. (1976) *The Power Game: An Examination of Decision Making in Government* (Macmillan).

Bullock, A. (1983) *Ernest Bevin: Foreign Secretary* (Heinemann).

Burridge, T. (1985) *Clement Attlee: A Political Biography* (Jonathan Cape).

Butler, D. (1989) *British General Elections since 1945* (Basil Blackwell).

Butler, D. and Pinto-Duschinsky, M. (1971) *The British General Election of 1970* (Macmillan).

Butler, R. (1973) *The Art of the Possible: The Memoirs of Lord Butler* (Penguin).

Callaghan, J. (1987) *Time and Chance* (Collins).

Carlton, D. (1981) *Anthony Eden* (Allen Lane).

Carlton, D. (1988) *Britain and the Suez Crisis* (Basil Blackwell).

Castle, B. (1980) *The Castle Diaries, 1974–6* (Weidenfeld and Nicolson).

Churchill, R. (1964) *The Fight for the Tory Leadership: A Contemporary Chronicle* (Heinemann).

Cockerell, M. (1988) *Live from No 10: The Inside Story of Prime Ministers and Television* (Faber and Faber).

Cockerell, M., Hennessy, P. and Walker, D. (1984) *Sources Close to the Prime Minister* (Macmillan).

Colville, J. (1985) *The Fringes of Power: Downing St. Diaries 1939–55* (Hodder and Stoughton).

Contemporary Record: The Journal of the Institute of Contemporary British History (Philip Allan).

Cosgrave, P. (1972) 'The Weakness of the Prime Minister' in W. J. Stankiewicz (ed.) (1976) *British Government in the Era of Reform* (Macmillan).

Cosgrave, P. (1985) *Carrington: A Life and Policy* (J. M. Dent).

Crossman, R. (1963), introduction to Walter Bagehot, *The English Constitution* (Collins).

Crossman, R. (1972) *Inside View: Three Lectures on Prime Ministerial Government* (Jonathan Cape).

Crossman, R. (1975, 1976, 1977) *The Diaries of a Cabinet Minister*, volumes I–III (Hamilton, and Jonathan Cape).

Donoughue B. (1987) *Prime Minister: The Conduct of Policy under Harold Wilson and James Callaghan* (Jonathan Cape).

Falkender, M. (1983) *Downing Street in Perspective* (Weidenfeld and Nicolson) (See also Williams, M.).

Gilbert, M. (1988) *Never Despair: Winston S. Churchill 1946–1965* (Heinemann).

Gowing, M. (1974) *Independence and Deterrence: Britain and Atomic Energy; Policy Making* (Macmillan).

Haines, J. (1977) *The Politics of Power* (Coronet Books).

Harris, K. (1982) *Attlee* (Weidenfeld and Nicolson).

Healey, D. (1989) *The Time of My Life* (Michael Joseph).

Henderson, N. (1984) *The Private Office* (Weidenfeld and Nicolson).

Hennessy, P. (1986) *Cabinet* (Basil Blackwell).

Hennessy, P. and Seldon, A. (eds) (1987) *Ruling Performance: British Governments from Attlee to Thatcher* (Basil Blackwell).

Holmes, M. (1985) *The Labour Government, .1974–79* (Macmillan).

Holmes, M. (1985) *The First Thatcher Government, 1979–83* (Wheatsheaf Books).

Home, A. Douglas- (1978) *The Way the Wind Blows: an Autobiography* (Fontana).

Horne, A. (1988) *Macmillan: 1894–1956* (Macmillan).

Horne, A. (1989) *Macmillan: 1957–1986* (Macmillan).

Hurd, D. (1979) *An End to Promises* (Collins).

Ingle, S. (1987) *The British Party System* (Basil Blackwell).

Jay, D. (1980) *Change and Fortune* (Hutchinson).

Jenkins, P. (1989) *Mrs Thatcher's Revolution: The Ending of the Socialist Era* (Pan Books).

Kavanagh, D. (1987) *Thatcherism and British Politics: The End of Consensus?* (Oxford University Press).

Kavanagh, D. and Morris, P. (1989) *Consensus Politics: From Attlee to Thatcher* (Basil Blackwell).

Kelly, R. (1989) *Conservative Party Conferences: the Hidden System* (Manchester University Press).

King, A. (ed.) (1969; 2nd edn 1985) *The British Prime Minister* (Macmillan).

Lamb, R. (1987) *The Failure of the Eden Government* (Sidgwick and Jackson).

McKenzie, R. (1955; 2nd edn 1963) *British Political Parties* (Heinemann).

Macmillan, H. (1971) *Riding the Storm, 1955–59* (Macmillan).

Macmillan, H. (1972) *Pointing the Way, 1959–61* (Macmillan).

Madgwick, P. J. (1984) *Introduction to British Politics* (Hutchinson).

Margach, J. (1978) *The Abuse of Power: The War between Downing Street and the Media* (W. H. Allen).

Margach, J. (1989) *The Anatomy of Power: An Enquiry into the Personality of Leadership* (W. H. Allen).

Minogue, K. and Biddiss, M. (eds) (1987) *Thatcherism: Personality and Politics* (Macmillan).

Morgan, K. O. (1984) *Labour in Power 1945–51* (Oxford University Press).

Nicholson, H. (1952) *King George The Fifth: His Life and Reign* (Constable).

Norton, P. and Aughey, A. (1981) *Conservatives and Conservatism* (Temple Smith).

Parliamentary Affairs.

Penniman, H. (1975) *Britain at the Polls: The Parliamentary Election of 1974* (American Enterprise Institute for Public Policy Research).

Public Administration.

Radcliffe, Lord (1976) *Report of the Committee of Privy Counsellors on Ministerial Memoirs*, Cmnd 6386.

Rhodes James, R. (1986) *Anthony Eden* (Weidenfeld and Nicolson).

Rose, R. and Suleiman, E. N. (1980) *Presidents and Prime Ministers* (American Enterprise Institute for Public Policy Research).

Seldon, A. (1981) *Churchill's Indian Summer: The Conservative Government, 1951—1955* (Hodder and Stoughton).

Shlaim, A. *et al.* (1977) *British Foreign Secretaries Since 1945* (David and Charles).

Shuckburgh, E. (1986) *Descent to Suez: Diaries 1951—56* (Weidenfeld and Nicolson).

Thorpe, D. (1989) *Selwyn Lloyd* (Jonathan Cape).

Whitelaw, W. (1989) *The Whitelaw Memoirs* (Headline).

Williams, M. (1972) *Inside Number 10* (Weidenfeld and Nicolson) (See also Falkender, M.).

Wilson, H. (1974) *The Labour Government 1964—70: A Personal Record* (Weidenfeld and Nicolson).

Wilson, H. (1979) *Final Term: the Labour Government, 1974—6* (Weidenfeld and Nicolson, Michael Joseph).

Young, H. (1989) *One of Us* (Macmillan).

Index